The Step-by-Step Guide to

PLANNING
YOUR WEDDING

Visit our How To website at www.howto.co.uk

At **www.howto.co.uk** you can engage in conversation with our authors – all of whom have 'been there and done that' in their specialist fields. You can get access to special offers and additional content but most importantly you will be able to engage with, and become a part of, a wide and growing community of people just like yourself.

At **www.howto.co.uk** you'll be able to talk and share tips with people who have similar interests and are facing similar challenges in their lives. People who, just like you, have the desire to change their lives for the better – be it through moving to a new country, starting a new business, growing their own vegetables, or writing a novel.

At **www.howto.co.uk** you'll find the support and encouragement you need to help make your aspirations a reality.

You can go direct to **www.step-by-step-guide-to-planning-your-wedding.co.uk** which is part of the main How To site.

How To Books strives to present authentic, inspiring, practical information in their books. Now, when you buy a title from **How To Books,** you get even more than just words on a page.

The Step-by-Step Guide to

PLANNING YOUR WEDDING

Lynda Wright

howtobooks

Published by How To Books Ltd,
Spring Hill House, Spring Hill Road,
Begbroke, Oxford OX5 1RX. United Kingdom.
Tel: (01865) 375794. Fax: (01865) 379162.
info@howtobooks.co.uk
www.howtobooks.co.uk

How To Books greatly reduce the carbon footprint of their books by sourcing their typesetting and printing in the UK.

British Library Cataloguing in Publication Data
A catalogue record for this book is available from the British Library

First published in 1994 by Checkmark Publications

ISBN 978 1 84528 410 7

Cartoons © Colin Shelbourn www.shelbourn.com
Produced for How To Books by Deer Park Productions, Tavistock, Devon
Typeset by PDQ Typesetting, Newcastle-under-Lyme, Staffs.
Printed and bound by Bell & Bain Ltd, Glasgow.

NOTE: The material contained in this book is set out in good faith for general guidance and no liability can be accepted for loss or expense incurred as a result of relying in particular circumstances on statements made in the book. The laws and regulations are complex and liable to change, and readers should check the current position with the relevant authorities before making personal arrangements.

CONTENTS

HOW TO USE THIS BOOK

Written and designed in a logical, easy-to-use style, the book covers every organisational detail from the day of the engagement right through to after the wedding or civil formation.

Concentrating totally on the practical aspects of the preparations, the book is divided into three sections – Wedding Countdown Calendar, Action Plans and Checklists. To obtain the maximum benefit from the book and to simplify your planning, it is recommended that you follow the suggested sequence:

1. Refer to the Countdown Calendar that lists all the vital steps at each stage of the preparations. The page numbers in brackets relate to the next section of the book – the Action Plans.

2. Follow the step-by-step sequence detailed in each Action Plan. In some instances this is supplemented by additional information.

3. Finally, turn to the Checklist section of the book to record all relevant information to enable you to track your progress at every vital step towards the wedding day or civil formation.

ENGAGEMENT

Although announcing an engagement is far less formal these days, it is still courteous for the man to seek the consent of the bride's parents and ensure that they have no objections to the marriage.

As soon as you get engaged, you'll be keen to tell as many relatives and friends as possible your exciting news. Make a list and decide how you want to tell them and whether you will have a party to celebrate.

❑ Inform both sets of parents at the earliest opportunity
❑ Consider what type of ring you would like
  - new   • second-hand   • specially-designed
  - re-set stone(s)
❑ Purchase the engagement ring
  Consider the type of wedding ring you will wear. The size of your hand and fingers should also influence your choice
❑ Arrange a celebration for both sets of parents
  - drinks   • lunch   • dinner
❑ Compile a list of relatives and close friends you wish to inform
  - visit   • letter   • telephone   • at a party

❑ Produce a schedule with the suggested columns

Name and Address	Tel. No.	Visit ✓	Letter ✓	Phone ✓	Party ✓	Done ✓

❑ Consider whether you wish to make a formal announcement
  • national newspaper   • local newspaper   • at a party or celebration
❑ Prepare the newspaper announcement
❑ Purchase party invitations
❑ Decide whether you wish to have an engagement portrait
❑ Prepare an engagement gift list
❑ Consider where you will store the gifts
❑ Write thank-you letters for gifts

WEDDING COUNTDOWN CALENDAR

It is difficult to state specifically the order in which you should plan and make all the necessary arrangements, since it will depend on the style of wedding or civil formation and the time available. However, it is advisable to make as early a start as possible to ensure you get exactly what you want and you are not rushed into making decisions.

The calendar is based on having at least six months to make all the arrangements and suggests possible timings. You may find it necessary to adapt the calendar in order to suit your individual needs or if you have less time available to make the preparations.

The page numbers in brackets refer to the relevant action plans. Specific responsibilities are shown as (B) Bride only and (G) Groom only; it is assumed that the remainder of the duties will be shared.

6–12 months
❑ Decide whether you wish to have a church wedding, a civil ceremony or marry abroad
❑ Decide on preference for date and time of ceremony
❑ Decide if you wish to have a Service of Blessing (page 64)

6–12 months (Cont.)

❏ Consider the number of guests, style of wedding and reception

❏ Prepare a provisional budget (page 19)

❏ Arrange a loan, if required (page 19)

❏ Make an appointment to see the officiant to book church ceremony (page 23)

❏ Make an appointment to see the officiant to book Service of Blessing (page 64)

❏ Arrange approved premises for civil ceremony or civil formation (pages 42 and 54)

❏ See the Superintendent Registrar or Civil Partnership Officer to provisionally book the civil ceremony (pages 45 and 55)
This can be arranged up to 12 months in advance

❏ Give notice of intended marriage or civil formation at appropriate register office(s) (pages 36 and 51)

❏ Make arrangements for marrying abroad (page 60)

❏ Choose best man, bridesmaids, pageboys, ushers and witnesses (page 169)

❏ Advise attendants of their respective duties (page 86)

❏ Arrange the reception venue (page 123)

❏ Arrange marquee (page 137)

❏ Arrange professional caterers (page 143)

❏ Arrange entertainment (page 157)

❏ Decide on the colour scheme of the wedding or ceremony

❏ Plan clothes for bride, especially if the dress is being made (B) (page 104)

❑ Plan clothes for groom and the other men in the wedding party (G) (page 113)

❑ Plan clothes for attendants, especially if any outfits are being made (pages 108–115)

❑ Book dressmaker and choose pattern(s) and fabric(s) (B) (page 105)

❑ Choose a milliner and shoemaker (B)

❑ Decide upon your honeymoon destination (page 162)

❑ Book the honeymoon and arrange travel insurance (page 162)

❑ Book florist (page 66)

❑ Book professional photographer and videographer (pages 68 and 71)

❑ Arrange transport for wedding day and going-away (page 74)

❑ Compose the guest list and have some names in reserve (page 76)

❑ Draw up a separate list for additional evening guests (page 76)

❑ Consider wedding gift options (page 81)

❑ Consider taking out an insurance policy to cover possible disasters

❑ Consider whether you wish to have a pre-nuptial agreement drawn up

5 months

❑ Meet the officiant to discuss arrangements for the church ceremony, particularly the order of service (page 25)

❑ Meet the organist to discuss the music (page 25)

5 months (Cont.)

❑ Book musicians and singers to perform during the ceremony (page 25)

❑ Order wedding invitations *(one per couple or family)* (page 78)

❑ Order printed order of service sheets *(one for each guest, officiant, organist and each member of the choir, plus mementoes)* (page 78)

❑ Identify items for your wedding gift list (page 81)

4 months

❑ Buy the wedding rings and arrange insurance cover (page 21)

❑ Obtain dates when the banns will be published (page 24)

❑ Arrange for the banns to be published in groom's church if different to the bride's church (page 24)

❑ Buy dress/headdress or outfit/hat if not being made or hired (B) (page 104)

❑ Arrange to hire or purchase clothes and accessories for the groom and the other men in the wedding party (G) (page 113)

3 months

❑ Advise reception venue or caterers of details regarding food, drink and approximate number of guests (page 123)

❑ Book any required staff *(toastmaster, cloakroom attendants, etc.)* (pages 128 and 147)

❑ Order the wedding cake or make your own (page 149)

❑ Register with store or online provider for gift or charity
   pledges (page 81)

❑ Prepare a wedding gift list or information pack (page 81)

❑ Prepare a map to send out with invitations and to have
   available after the ceremony. Show location of the ceremony,
   reception venue, car parking and stations, with a suggested
   route from the ceremony to the reception

❑ Plan your beauty régime (B) (page 117)

❑ Check that existing passports are in order and arrange a new
   passport in married name, if required (B) (page 162)

❑ Find out about any inoculations and visas required for the
   honeymoon

❑ Visit your doctor or family planning clinic for a check-up and
   advice (B)

2 months

❑ Finalise the guest list

❑ Send out invitations at least six weeks before the wedding and
   list acceptances and refusals as they arrive (page 76)

❑ Acknowledge invitation replies and include a wedding gift list
   or information pack, the map and, where appropriate, a list of
   nearby hotels and guesthouses with prices (page 76)

❑ Write thank-you letters for gifts or donations as they arrive and
   record details (page 83)

❑ Order wedding stationery, balloons, bridal favours, crackers,
   etc. (page 78)

2 months (Cont.)

❏ If self-catering, make detailed plans and begin cooking for the freezer (page 139)
❏ Purchase gift for the bride (G) and groom (B)
❏ Purchase gifts for the best man and attendants (page 84)
❏ Book accommodation for your wedding night
❏ Choose and buy your shoes, underwear and accessories (B)
❏ Buy going-away outfits, clothes and luggage for the honeymoon

4 weeks

❏ Check bookings for the ceremony, florist, photographer, video company, transport, reception venue, entertainment and the wedding cake
❏ Agree a date with the officiant for the wedding rehearsal and notify all the people concerned
❏ Arrange final fitting of wedding dress (*wear appropriate underwear and shoes*) (B)
❏ Arrange appointment for final fitting of bridesmaids' and pageboys' outfits
❏ Make arrangements for the wedding report to appear in newspaper
❏ Discuss with attendants where they will dress on the wedding day
❏ Visit hairdresser with your veil and headdress and discuss hairstyle (B)

❑ Make an appointment with your hairdresser for the wedding day (B)

❑ Practise your wedding day make-up (B)

❑ Arrange any pre-wedding parties and the stag and hen parties (page 161)

❑ Arrange hospitality and transport for any out-of-town guests (page 159)

❑ Check the honeymoon arrangements and tickets (page 162)

❑ Make arrangements for pets with neighbours or boarding out

❑ Arrange any necessary inoculations and medicines

3 weeks

❑ Chase up any outstanding invitation replies and finalise the guest list

❑ Prepare the seating plan and place name cards

❑ Order currency and travellers' cheques for the honeymoon

❑ Prepare speech for the reception (G)

2 weeks

❑ Inform the reception venue or caterers of final number of guests

❑ Arrange appointments with the photographer and videographer to finalise the arrangements (pages 68 and 71)

❑ Advise the florist of final number of buttonholes required

❑ Apply the icing if you have made your own cake

❑ Have engagement ring cleaned (B)

2 weeks (Cont.)
❑ Check that the bride's father and best man have prepared their speeches

1 week
❑ Check arrangements for the reception, advise final numbers and any special dietary requirements
❑ Make final check on arrangements for the flowers, transport, caterers and entertainment
❑ Decorate the cake or arrange to view it at professional bakers
❑ Hold the wedding rehearsal with all attendants *(church only)*
❑ Send announcement to the newspaper and make arrangements for report and photograph to be sent to the newspaper after the wedding
❑ Wrap gifts for attendants and plan when to give them
❑ Attend meetings with the photographer and videographer to finalise the arrangements
❑ Collect banns certificate from groom's officiant and pay fees
❑ Produce a list of the family and any guests who are to be personally escorted to their seats and any special seating arrangements at the ceremony
❑ Ensure all attendants know their duties, timings and venues
❑ Final check on clothing and try on whole outfit (B)
❑ Wear in wedding shoes at home (B)
❑ Attend final dress fitting of your attendants' clothes (B)
❑ Make arrangements for the return of any hired items
❑ Attend appointment with hairdresser (B)

❑ Have hair cut (G)

❑ Hold stag and hen parties

❑ Start assembling items for the honeymoon and do any last
minute shopping

❑ Make final check on the honeymoon arrangements

❑ Deliver order of service sheets to church for officiant, organist
and choir if not being collected by the chief usher on the
wedding day

❑ Check that car has petrol, oil and water and is in good working
order if you plan to use it for going away or the honeymoon
(G)

2/3 days

❑ Plan schedule for the wedding day with timings (pages 14
and 15)

❑ Collect any hired items of clothing and accessories

❑ Give the best man cash for church, Registrar's or Civil
Partnership Officer's fees and tips on the day, plus a spare set
of keys for the going-away car (G)

❑ Collect currency and travellers' cheques

1 day

❑ Continue preparations if self-catering
de-frost food and do last-minute shopping for perishables
assemble all equipment and glassware, chill wine, etc.
arrange furniture, lay tables and set up wedding gift table

❑ Assemble the cake for reception at home or deliver to venue

1 day (Cont.)

☐ Arrange display of wedding gifts at the reception

☐ Pack going-away clothes and have suitcase taken to reception venue

☐ Complete packing clothes for the honeymoon and assemble all tickets, passports and documents. Ensure luggage is at appropriate place of departure for the honeymoon

☐ Check that the going-away car is at the reception

☐ Hand gifts to the best man and attendants

☐ Have money available for tips and gratuities (G)

☐ Lay out wedding dress or outfit, accessories and jewellery (B)

☐ Assemble make-up, tissues, safety pins, etc. (B) (page 121)

☐ Have manicure and pedicure (B)

☐ Wash hair if not going to hairdresser (B)

☐ Relax and have an early night

On the day (B)
Time

_____ Shower or bath

_____ Try to eat a substantial breakfast

_____ Wash hair*

_____ Leave for hairdresser* (*delete as appropriate)

_____ Apply make-up (after washing hair or going to hairdresser)

_____ Polish fingernails or repair as necessary

_____ Best man arrives to collect your honeymoon luggage and any greetings cards, emails or telemessages to be read out at reception

_____ Chief usher to collect buttonholes, order of service sheets
and maps

_____ Bridesmaids and pageboys to arrive

_____ Put on dress, veil and headdress or outfit and hat

_____ Photographer arrives

_____ Videographer arrives

_____ Car(s) arrive

_____ Arrive for the ceremony 10 minutes before it begins
(civil ceremony only)

_____ Ceremony begins

_____ Photographs

_____ Reception receiving line

_____ Meal begins

_____ Speeches

_____ Evening reception begins

_____ Change into going-away outfit

_____ Leave for overnight destination or honeymoon

On the day (G)
Time

_____ Shower or bath

_____ Dress

_____ Have speech available

_____ Meet the best man

_____ Check on rings and fees

_____ Arrive at the church, register office or approved premises
20 minutes before the ceremony begins

On the day (G) (Cont.)
Time

_____ Ceremony begins

_____ Photographs

_____ Reception receiving line

_____ Meal begins

_____ Speeches

_____ Evening reception begins

_____ Change into going-away outfit

_____ Leave for overnight destination or honeymoon

WHO PAYS FOR WHAT

Traditionally, the costs are divided as indicated below. Nowadays there is more flexibility and who meets the costs may vary as many couples opt to share all the costs or even pay for everything themselves.

The Bride
- Bridegroom's wedding ring
- Wedding gift for the bridegroom
- Beauty treatments and hairdressing
- Hen party
- Going-away outfit

The Bride's Family
- Press announcements
- Bride's dress and accessories
- Bridesmaids' and pageboys' clothes *(the cost may be shared with their parents)*
- Stationery items, including invitations and order of service sheets
- Transport to the ceremony *(except groom and best man)* and to the reception
- Flowers for the ceremony and reception
- Photographs and video recording
- Reception venue, catering and the wedding cake

The Bridegroom

- Engagement ring
- Bride's wedding ring
- Wedding gift for the bride
- Stag party
- Going-away transport
- Honeymoon

The Bridegroom's Family

- Bridegroom's outfit and accessories
- Ushers' outfits
- Church or Registrar's fees *(including organist, choir, singers, musicians and bell-ringers)*
- Flowers for the bride and bridesmaids, buttonholes and corsages
- Gifts for the bridesmaids, pageboys, best man and ushers
- Transport for the groom and best man to the ceremony and, possibly, for the bride and groom after the ceremony
- Out-of-pocket expenses for the best man

WEDDING EXPENSES

Once you are ready to embark on planning the wedding, the process of making lots of choices gets under way. It is essential to list all the likely expenses and budget for each one carefully. In deciding who will pay for what, a budget can be set and a likely total cost determined.

Refer to Checklist 2 'Wedding Expenses', page 172

❑ Agree a provisional budget and decide how expenses will be allocated between the bride and groom and the respective parents. As actual costs become available, you may wish to enter these on the Checklist to provide a complete, up-to-date record

❑ Compile a list of all likely expenses associated with your wedding requirements

❑ Consider whether you will need a loan
  Arrange this well in advance, preferably with approval in principle, so you only need draw on it if and when required

❑ Allow plenty of time to shop around and check websites to compare prices

❑ Contact suppliers to obtain an idea of prices and request brochures or literature on the goods and services you require

❑ Draw up detailed specifications for goods and services required and send to relevant suppliers. An identical specification should be sent to each particular group of suppliers to enable accurate comparisons

❑ Compare the estimates or quotations
Estimates provide only an approximate idea of the final cost, whereas quotations usually state fixed prices

❑ Check whether VAT is payable and that all amounts include delivery charges, staff costs, etc. Enquire whether there is a time limit on acceptance and that the figures will not be affected by any future price increases

❑ Modify your requirements or budget if estimates or quotations exceed available funds

❑ Request written detailed agreements for supplies and services

❑ Read and fully understand any contracts for goods and services before you add your signature. Carefully check any wording in small print and ensure commitments by any party are clearly set out

❑ Pay deposits as and when required
It is reasonable for a supplier to request a deposit, but it is important to check the procedure in the event of cancellation

❑ Settle outstanding balances at the appropriate time

WEDDING RINGS

The wedding ring, the traditional symbol of marriage, is exchanged during the wedding ceremony. Wedding rings do not need to be expensive or lavish as they represent the love and commitment you have for one another and the partnership into which you are entering.

Refer to Checklist 3 'Wedding Rings', page 184

❑ Purchase bride's wedding ring
   Choose one to complement your engagement ring. The size of your hand and fingers, and the possibility of wearing an eternity ring, should also influence your choice
❑ Purchase groom's wedding ring
❑ Obtain a jeweller's valuation certificate if you buy a ring from an antique shop or it is a family heirloom
❑ Decide whether to have the ring(s) engraved
   • wedding date
   • initials
   • a personal message
❑ Arrange a date for collection and pay any required deposit
❑ Arrange insurance cover
   You may find it useful to take a photograph or make a sketch of your engagement and wedding rings and note any inscriptions, hallmarks, number of stones and the setting. Keep receipts for the rings in the event of an insurance claim

❑ Have engagement ring cleaned before the wedding
*Rings should be regularly checked for any loose stones and
professionally cleaned from time to time*

CHURCH WEDDING

It is possible to have a church wedding whatever your beliefs and whether or not you are baptised and go to church. Marrying in church has never been easier thanks to a change in the law, which means you now have more churches to choose from. Lots of people marry in their own local church, but maybe you would like to marry in a church away from where you live because it has special significance for you through family or other connections.

Refer to Checklist 4 'Church Wedding', page 186

❑ Make an appointment with the officiant to discuss the following details:
- date and time of ceremony
- content and order of service – *see 'Order of Service', page 25*
- bell-ringers, organist and choir and the relevant cost
- suggest a meeting with the organist and obtain a contact telephone number
- check whether there are any other weddings on the same day
- flowers and who will provide them
  Some churches provide flowers and you may need to specify the type and colour required. If so, ascertain whether you will be required to contribute towards the cost. You may also wish to liaise with any other couples getting married on the same day

- permission for photography and video recording
- the policy regarding confetti
- amount of church fees and details of payment
- dates for wedding preparation classes or instruction
- dates when the banns will be published *(on three Sundays before the wedding)*
- date for the rehearsal with all attendants present
- obtain signature on the necessary form if you wish to change the name in your passport before the wedding

❏ Make an appointment with the organist to discuss the music – *see 'Order of Service', page 25*

❏ Arrange for the banns to be published in groom's church if different to the bride's church

❏ Choose at least two witnesses *(this is a legal requirement)*

❏ Make a sketch of the inside of the church if required by photographer, videographer, etc.

❏ Ascertain location and quantity of parking space for guests' cars

ORDER OF SERVICE

Choosing the music and readings is all part of personalising your big day.

Refer to Checklist 5 'Order of Service', page 188

❑ Discuss the content and order of service with the officiant. Seek their advice and, if possible, refer to order of service sheets from previous weddings
  - discuss inclusion of Holy Communion/Nuptial Mass
  - discuss version of service and vows
  - state any preferences
    - for the Reading(s) – see 'Music and Bible Readings', page 27
    - for the Prayers
    - for any specific points to be mentioned in the Address
  - seek approval to include any performances
    - by the choir
    - by singer(s)
    - by musician(s)
  - discuss the hymns, psalms and organ music you would like – *see 'Music and Bible Readings', page 27*

❑ Arrange to meet the organist
  - discuss the music you would like played. *It may be helpful to purchase or borrow a CD or download relevant tracks*
    - as a medley before the service begins

      – for the entrance of the bride *(Processional)*

      – during the signing of the register

      – leaving the church *(Recessional)*

- offer to obtain sheet music, if appropriate
- discuss your choice of hymns/psalms
- determine how many order of service sheets are required for the choir

❑ Book singer(s) and musician(s)

❑ Decide whether you will print the words or use hymn books

MUSIC AND BIBLE READINGS

Music can play an important part in your wedding as it sets the tone, creates an atmosphere and helps make the day more memorable for everyone. It is advisable to keep readings fairly short and to choose hymns that the majority of your guests will recognise and can join in singing.

Processional Music
As the bride walks up the aisle
- Bridal March from Lohengrin – Wagner
- Fugue in G Minor – Bach
- Grand March from Aida – Verdi
- Hornpipe in D from the Water Music – Handel
- Prelude from Te Deum – Charpentier
- Prince of Denmark's March – Clarke
- The Arrival of the Queen of Sheba – Handel
- Toccata in C – Zipoli
- Trumpet Minuet – Hollins
- Trumpet Tune and Air -Purcell
- Trumpet Tune in D – Stanley
- Trumpet Voluntary – Clarke
- Wedding Fanfare – Bliss
- Wedding March from The Marriage of Figaro – Mozart

Traditional Hymns

Allow for up to three hymns

❏ Alleluia, sing to Jesus
❏ All people that on earth do dwell
❏ All things bright and beautiful
❏ And did those feet in ancient time (Jerusalem)
❏ At the name of Jesus every knee shall bow
❏ Come down, O Love divine
❏ Dear Lord and Father of mankind
❏ Father, hear the prayer we offer
❏ Glorious things of thee are spoken
❏ Great is thy faithfulness
❏ Guide me, O thou great Redeemer
❏ I vow to thee, my country
❏ Immortal, invisible, God only wise
❏ Lead us, heavenly Father, lead us
❏ Let all the world in every corner sing
❏ Lord of all hopefulness, Lord of all joy
❏ Love divine, all loves excelling
❏ Now thank we all our God
❏ O for a thousand tongues to sing
❏ O Jesus I have promised
❏ O Lord my God when I in awesome wonder
❏ O perfect Love, all human thought transcending
❏ O praise ye the Lord
❏ Praise, my soul, the King of Heaven
❏ Praise to the Lord, the Almighty, the King of creation

❑ Rejoice the Lord is King
❑ The King of love my Shepherd is
❑ The Lord is my Shepherd (Psalm 23) – to the tune of Crimond
❑

Modern Popular Hymns

❑ Amazing Grace
❑ Be still for the presence of the Lord
❑ Bind us together
❑ Come on and celebrate
❑ From heaven you came helpless babe (The Servant King)
❑ Give me joy in my heart
❑ Give thanks with a grateful heart
❑ I cannot tell why he whom angels worship
❑ Jesus is Lord! Creation's voice proclaims it
❑ Jesus put this song into our hearts
❑ Jesus, stand among us at the meeting of our lives
❑ Let there be love shared among us
❑ Lord Jesus Christ, you have come to us
❑ Lord for the years your love has kept and guided
❑ Lord the light of your love is shining (Shine, Jesus, shine)
❑ Make me a channel of your peace
❑ Morning has broken
❑ New every morning is the love
❑ Lord of the Dance
❑ One more step along the world I go
❑ Tell out my soul

❏ You shall go out with joy

❏

Favourite Psalms

❏ 23: The Lord is my Shepherd

❏ 48: Great is the Lord, and highly to be praised

❏ 67: God be merciful unto us, and bless us

❏ 121: I will lift up mine eyes unto the hills

❏ 127: Except the Lord build the house

❏ 128: Blessed is everyone that feareth the Lord

❏

Readings
Old Testament

❏ Genesis – Chapter 1, verses 26–28 and 31a

❏ Song of Solomon – Chapter 2, verses 10–13 and Chapter 8, verses 6 and 7

❏ Jeremiah – Chapter 31, verses 31–34

❏ Tobit – Chapter 8, verses 4–8

❏

New Testament

❏ Matthew – Chapter 5, verses 1–10

❏ Matthew – Chapter 7, verses 21, 24–27

❏ Mark – Chapter 10, verses 6–9 and verses 13–16

❏ John – Chapter 2, verses 1–11

❏ John – Chapter 15, verses 1–8

❑ John – Chapter 15, verses 9–17
❑ Romans – Chapter 7, verses 1, 2, 9–18
❑ Romans – Chapter 8, verses 31–35, 37–39
❑ Romans – Chapter 12, verses 1, 2, 9–13
❑ Romans – Chapter 15, verses 1–3, 5–7, 13
❑ 1 Corinthians – Chapter 13
❑ Ephesians – Chapter 3, verses 14–end
❑ Ephesians – Chapter 4, verses 1–6
❑ Ephesians – Chapter 5, verses 21–end
❑ Philippians – Chapter 4, verses 4–9
❑ Colossians – Chapter 3, verses 12–17
❑ 1 John – Chapter 3, verses 18–end
❑ 1 John – Chapter 4, verses 7–12
❑

Signing the Register
❑ Adagio from Toccata, Adagio and Fugue in C – Bach
❑ Air and Gavotte – Wesley
❑ Air from the Water Music – Handel
❑ Canon in D major – Pachelbel
❑ Jesu, Joy of Man's Desiring – Bach
❑ Largo from the New World Symphony – Dvorak
❑ Pastoral Symphony from The Messiah – Handel
❑ Pastorale to a Wild Rose – Macdowell
❑ Prelude from Greensleeves – Vaughan-Williams
❑ Prelude from Prelude, Fugue and Variation Op 18 – Franck

❏ Sheep May Safely Graze – Bach

Recessional Music

As the bride and groom leave the church together
❏ Allegro from Symphony No. 6 – Widor
❏ Bridal March – Hollins
❏ Choral Song – Wesley
❏ Fanfare – Whitlock
❏ Music for the Royal Fireworks – Handel
❏ Pomp and Circumstance March No. 4 – Elgar
❏ The 'Great' G major Prelude – Bach
❏ Toccata from Symphony No. 5 – Widor
❏ Toccata in C – Pachelbel
❏ Trumpet Voluntary – Clarke
❏ Wedding March from A Midsummer Night's Dream –
Mendelssohn

CIVIL CEREMONY

The options available will enable you to have the type of ceremony you wish at the location of your choice. You can either have a simple ceremony with just two witnesses or a ceremony where the bride is given away and bridesmaids/pageboys attend. You may have music and readings, but any with slight religious overtones need to be agreed with the Registrar before the day of Marriage. It is unlikely that you will be allowed to have live music, although you will be allowed to have approved recorded music to be played on either your own (or hired) system or the register office's system.

The choice of venue is also yours. You can get married at any register office in England or Wales or in approved premises, which are licensed by local authorities.

You will appreciate the benefit of this flexibility:

- if your local register office is not able to accommodate the number of guests you wish to invite
- if you have moved away from an area, but would like to return there to get married
- if you desire a more unusual and memorable venue.

However, the wedding still has to take place indoors, between 8 a.m. and 6 p.m., with two adult witnesses present. These may be relatives, friends or colleagues who must be able to speak and understand English. *Refer to the General Register Office website (www.gro.gov.uk) for further information.*

SCOTLAND

Regulations on marriage are much less restrictive than in England and Wales. Couples are able to get married anywhere they like, even out-of-doors or at home, subject to approval by the local council. The legal age is 16 or over and the permission of parents or guardian is not required.

Both parties must inform the Registrar of their intention to marry and submit their completed marriage notice forms, relevant documents, declarations and fees to the Registrar of Marriages in the District where the marriage is to take place. There are no residency requirements and notice must be given in the three-month period prior to the date of the marriage and should be with the Registrar four weeks before the marriage. If either party has been married before, the notices should be with the Registrar six weeks before. The minimum period is fifteen days before the date of the proposed marriage.

Although both parties need not attend personally at the Registrar's Office to hand in their marriage notice, at least one of the couple must attend there personally before the date of the marriage to finalise the arrangements.

While nothing of a religious nature may be included in the ceremony, it is possible to have music, poetry, exchange of rings, etc. and this should be discussed with the Registrar, as should any flower arrangements. *Refer to the General Register Office for Scotland website* (www.gro-scotland.gov.uk) for further information.

NORTHERN IRELAND

The legal age is 16 or over and persons over 16 and under 18 require the consent of parents or guardian. There are no residency requirements and notice must be given in the 12-month period prior to the date of the marriage and should be with the Registrar eight weeks before the marriage. If either party has been married before, the notices should be with the Registrar ten weeks before. The minimum period is 14 days before the date of the proposed marriage.

Both parties must inform the Registrar of their intention to marry and submit their completed marriage notice forms, relevant documents, declarations and fees to the Registrar of Marriages in the District where the marriage is to take place. The notice forms may be submitted in person or by post to the Registrar. The parties may be requested to attend at the Registrar's Office to finalise the arrangements, and/or collect the marriage schedule.

Whilst nothing of a religious nature may be included in the ceremony, it is possible to have music, poetry, exchange of rings, etc. and this should be discussed with the Registrar, as should any flower arrangements. *Refer to the General Register Office (Northern Ireland) website (www.groni.gov.uk) for further information.*

LEGAL PRELIMINARIES

It is a legal requirement for both to give notice of intention to marry. You cannot give more than one year's notice of your intention to marry. The notice is a legal document that must be given and signed by each of the people getting married.

MARRIAGE BY CERTIFICATE

- You must both have lived in any district in England and Wales for at least seven days immediately before giving notice of intention to marry. It does not matter if either of you moves to a different address after the notice has been given.
- If you live in a different district from the person you are marrying, you can choose to marry in the register office in the district where either of you live or in any register office of your choice. Notice must be given to the Superintendent Registrar in each district.
- If you both live in the same district, notice must be given by both of you.
- However, it is important to first contact the district where you wish the marriage to take place.
- Once you have given notice you must wait 15 clear days before the marriage can take place. You can collect your

certificate for the marriage in the district (or districts) in which the notice was given as soon as this waiting period is over. The certificate is the legal document that allows your marriage to take place.

- The certificate should be presented to the Registrar of the district where the marriage is to take place.
- The marriage may then take place at any time within 12 months from the day on which you gave notice.

DESIGNATED OFFICE SYSTEM

This relates to a marriage involving someone who is subject to immigration control. Initially a letter must be obtained from the Home Office stating they can marry in the UK. They then need to give formal notice to a Designated Office. The details of such notices will change if one or both of the parties to a marriage are subject to immigration control and also the location of the persons and their Designated Office. The Home Office or the Superintendent Registrar can supply these details and a list of the Designated Offices in England and Wales.

THE NECESSARY DOCUMENTS

When giving notice of marriage, you will be asked to produce evidence of identity and nationality – preferably your passport or birth certificate – and proof of residence, e.g. an electricity or telephone bill. With a birth certificate, another form of identification is required – driving licence, medical card, ID card or nationality document stating date of birth.

It is important to note that certain documents will be required if any of the following circumstances apply:

- proof of your parent's or guardian's approval if you are under 18. The relevant form can be obtained from the register office
- evidence of how your most recent marriage ended if you have been married before:
  - in the case of divorce, your Decree Absolute bearing an original stamp from the issuing court, with an English translation if appropriate
  - if you have been widowed, the death certificate of your former spouse
- a passport, Home Office Document or other official identity document, with an English translation if appropriate, if born outside the UK
- Deed Poll, Change of Name Deed or Statutory Declaration if you have changed your name.

FEES

Fees are set nationally by Parliament for register office ceremonies held in England and Wales and are regularly reviewed.

A fee will be payable for:

- giving the notices of a wedding; this is per person in each register office where notice is given
- conducting the marriage ceremony and one copy of the marriage certificate *(this fee is payable on the wedding day, so be sure to have cash available)*.

CIVIL MARRIAGE IN APPROVED PREMISES

Each local register office holds a list of approved premises in its district. These include banqueting suites, hotels, stately homes and other buildings of historical interest. More unusual venues include London Zoo, Pinewood Film Studios, Coventry City Football Club, Sandown Park Racecourse and HMS Warrior, Portsmouth.

If you have a civil ceremony at approved premises, the Registrar will charge a higher fee to take into account the additional administration, time and costs involved in travelling to the venue. The fee will also vary depending on whether the ceremony is to be held on a weekday, Saturday, Sunday or Bank Holiday and is payable in advance. Although these charges are set locally, they tend not to vary significantly from area to area.

The law does not allow for civil marriages to be held in the open air, in a tent or marquee, in any other movable structure such as a boat or a hot air balloon, nor in any building that has present or past connection with any religion.

Some venues can only hold the wedding ceremony and you will have to find another venue for the reception. At other venues it is negotiable and some will only allow the ceremony if you have a reception as well. In any case, you should contact the manager or owner of the premises to make provisional arrangements before contacting the register office.

- Notice of intended marriage must be given in the district(s) where you both live and the certificate presented to the register office in the district where the ceremony is to be held if they are not the same.
- The same residency rules of seven clear days apply.
- The marriage may take place at any time within 12 months from the day on which notice was given.

SUGGESTIONS FOR MUSIC

Frank Sinatra Classics
❑ Hello young lovers
❑ Let's fall in love
❑ Somebody loves me

The Beatles No. 1 Singles
❑ Love me do
❑ I want to hold your hand
❑ Can't buy me love
❑ All you need is love

Various Artists
❑ Angels – Robbie Williams
❑ Love is all around – Wet Wet Wet
❑ I'll never break your heart – Backstreet Boys
❑ I love you always forever – Donna Lewis
❑ One moment in time – Whitney Houston
❑ If you don't know me by now – Simply Red

- ❏ Have I told you lately – Rod Stewart
- ❏ How deep is your love – Bee Gees
- ❏ It must be love – Madness
- ❏ I'll never fall in love again – Deacon Blue
- ❏ Show me heaven – Maria McKee
- ❏ Wonderful tonight – Eric Clapton
- ❏ Romeo and Juliet – Dire Straits
- ❏ Power of love – Jennifer Rush
- ❏ Always on my mind – Elvis Presley

SUGGESTIONS FOR POETRY AND READINGS

- ❏ I wanna be yours by John Cooper Clarke
- ❏ Shall I compare thee to a summer's day? (Sonnet 18) by William Shakespeare
- ❏ How do I love thee? Let me count the ways (Sonnet From the Portugese) by Elizabeth Barrett Browning
- ❏ Songs from the Princess by Alfred, Lord Tennyson
- ❏ Come live with me, and be my love (The Passionate Shepherd to His Love) by Christopher Marlowe
- ❏ He wishes for cloths of heaven by W B Yeats
- ❏ The good morrow by John Donne

MARRYING ABROAD

Some countries require a Certificate of No Impediment. This is used for persons marrying in a foreign country where one of the parties is British and the other is a foreign national. Advice can be sought from a Superintendent Registrar or the Foreign Office.

A Superintendent Registrar may accept notice for a marriage to take place in a foreign country between a British subject and either a foreign subject or another British subject. He/she will be able to issue a certificate that can be produced to help the procedure abroad. However, the rules vary and you should consult the Superintendent Registrar.

Where a marriage is solemnised in a foreign country under local law, it is sometimes possible for a record of the marriage to be made under the Foreign Marriage Order 1970. This is not always the case and you should consult the Superintendent Registrar for more details.

CIVIL CEREMONY – REGISTER OFFICE

The choice of venue is yours as you can get married at any register office in England or Wales. Obtain addresses from local authorities, telephone directories or the Internet.

Refer to Checklist 6 'Civil Ceremony – Register Office', page 190

❑ Identify the register office of your choice
❑ Telephone the register office to provisionally book the ceremony
 This can be arranged up to 12 months in advance
❑ Call in person at the appropriate register office(s) to give notices of your intentions to marry and to pay the fees for giving notices – *see 'Marriage by Certificate', page 36*. It will

be necessary to produce evidence of identity for both parties
– *see 'The Necessary Documents', page 37*
❏ Make an appointment with the Superintendent Registrar to
discuss the following details:
- confirm the date and time of ceremony
- how many guests can be accommodated
- type of ceremony – standard or enhanced with the addition
of extra slightly religious declarations or poetry readings of
your choice
- the policy on playing appropriate music of your choice
providing it has only slight religious connotations
- the possibility of including the bride being 'given away'
- the policy on confetti, photography and video recording
- the possibility of having the ceremony broadcast live on the
internet and the cost
- provision of flowers
*A silk flower arrangement will be provided or you can
arrange to supply your own flowers*
- location and quantity of parking space for guests' cars
- amount of fees and details of payment
- obtain signature on the necessary form if you wish to
change the name in your passport before the wedding
❏ Choose at least two adult witnesses *(this is a legal
requirement)*
❏ Decide whether you wish to have a church Service of Blessing,
either directly after the marriage or on another day – *see
'Service of Blessing', page 64*

CIVIL CEREMONY – APPROVED PREMISES

*Many stately homes, prestigious buildings, hotels and restaurants –
all of which make great backdrops for your wedding photographs
– are licensed to hold weddings. You can obtain details of
approved venues from local register offices or on the Internet.*

**Refer to Checklist 7 'Civil Ceremony – Approved Premises',
page 192**

❏ Decide whether you prefer to have just the ceremony or both
the ceremony and reception at the venue
❏ Identify approved venues in the required area
❏ Enquire whether they offer facilities for the wedding alone or
both the wedding and reception
❏ Establish compatibility of venue with proposed style of
wedding
❏ Request brochures and prices
❏ Ascertain their hire charges for the room(s) and whether they
offer exclusive use of the venue and the cost
❏ Establish availability
  • date
  • time
  • room(s) *(depending on the number of guests)*
❏ Choose at least two adult witnesses *(this is a legal
requirement)*
❏ Decide whether you wish to have a church Service of Blessing,
either directly after the marriage or on another day – *see
'Service of Blessing', page 64*

Booking the Superintendent Registrar

❑ Telephone the register office to provisionally book the Superintendent Registrar
This can be arranged up to 12 months in advance

❑ Call in person at the appropriate register office(s) to give notices of your intentions to marry and to pay the fees for giving notices – *see 'Marriage by Certificate', page 36*. It will be necessary to produce evidence of identity for both parties – *see 'The Necessary Documents', page 37*

❑ Make an appointment with the Superintendent Registrar to discuss the following details:
  • confirm the date and time of ceremony
  • proposed venue
  • number of guests attending
  • type of ceremony – standard or enhanced with the addition of extra slightly religious declarations or poetry readings of your choice
  • the policy on playing appropriate music of your choice providing it has only slight religious connotations
  • the possibility of including the bride being 'given away'
  • the policy on confetti, photography and video recording
  • amount of fees and details of payment
  • obtain signature on the necessary form if you wish to change the name in your passport before the wedding

Booking a venue for the Wedding Ceremony only

❑ Make an appointment with the Venue Manager to discuss your requirements:
  - confirm the date and time of ceremony
  - number of guests attending
  - ask whether there are any other weddings on the same day
  - check on easy access for any elderly or disabled guests
  - provision of flowers
    Specify the type and colour if you wish the venue to provide them or you may prefer to ask your own florist
  - the policy on confetti
  - location and quantity of parking space for guests' cars
  - discuss the estimated cost and ascertain whether VAT is included
  - request a detailed estimate in writing

❑ Confirm acceptance in writing and enclose the required deposit

❑ One week before the wedding
  - telephone or call round to check the final arrangements
  - confirm the final number of guests

Booking a venue for the Wedding Ceremony and Reception

❑ See 'Booking a venue for the Wedding Ceremony only' above
❑ Refer to 'Reception', page 123

CIVIL PARTNERSHIP

The Civil Partnership Act 2004 gives same sex couples in the UK the right to register their partnership and acquire a new legal status as 'registered civil partners'. This includes rights pertaining to partner's children, taxation, inheritance, pensions and next-of-kin, such as registering a death, bereavement benefits, compensation in the event of a fatal accident and the right to stay living in a shared rented home.

There is no requirement for couples to say particular contractual words as part of the registration process nor will there be any legal necessity for any form of ceremony. The minimum requirement for the civil partnership ceremony will be the couple attending before an authorised Civil Partnership Officer and signing the schedule in the presence of two witnesses.

If the couple wish to have a ceremony around the signing of the schedule, which makes the formation, they need to discuss this with the Civil Partnership Officer, who will be present at the venue or register office.

A civil partnership is formed when the proposed civil partners sign the relevant document in the presence of an authorised Civil Partnership Officer and two witnesses. The civil partnership comes into being once the second civil partner signs the document. *Refer to the General Register website (www.gro.gov.uk) for information.*

SCOTLAND

Unlike England and Wales, it is not necessary to have parental permission to register a civil partnership while aged 16 or 17, nor to be resident in Scotland to register a civil partnership. People from outside the European Economic Area (the EU plus Norway, Iceland and Lichtenstein) or Switzerland need to obtain permission from the immigration authorities to register a civil partnership.

To register a civil partnership, both partners must submit a civil partnership notice to the District Registrar and this can be done by post. A date for registration is arranged with the Registrar – this must be at least 15 clear days after the date the notices are submitted. Registration involves a non-religious ceremony, which both the couple, and two witnesses over 16 years of age, must attend. While nothing of a religious nature may be included in the ceremony, it is possible to have music, poetry, exchange of rings, etc. and this should be discussed with the Registrar, as should any flower arrangements. The legal effects of civil partnership start as soon as the civil partnership schedule is signed at the ceremony.

Registration can take place at a registration office, or at any other place agreed with the local authority – the General Register

Office for Scotland publishes a list of places approved for registering a civil marriage, and most of these places should also be available for registering a civil partnership. If the place you want to use is not on the approved list, speak to the District Registrar for the relevant district. The main exception is religious premises: like civil marriage, a civil partnership cannot be registered on religious premises. However, a couple can have a blessing of their relationship on religious premises immediately before or after signing the register at a nearby location. *Refer to the General Register Office for Scotland website* (www.gro-scotland.gov.uk) for further information.

NORTHERN IRELAND

Both persons are required to be at least 16 years of age on the day of the civil partnership registration. Persons over 16 and under 18 need the consent of parents or a guardian. Two persons, 16 or over, need to be present to act as witnesses.

The ceremony may take place in a Registrar's Office or at an approved place. Details of approved places may be obtained from the Registrar of the District where the civil partnership is being registered or the General Register Office for Northern Ireland. Alternatively, you can apply to the Registrar of the District in which the civil partnership will be registered for a temporary approval at a place of your own choice, such as your own home. The Registrar will give advice regarding the fee and the application procedure.

By law, each party to a proposed civil partnership registration is required to complete a Civil Partnership Notice Form. These have to be submitted to the Registrar of the District where the registration is to take place, together with the relevant documents, declarations and fees, either in person or by post. Notice must be given in the 12-month period prior to the date of the registration and should be with the Registrar eight weeks before the ceremony. If either party has been married before or has entered a previous civil partnership, the notices should be with the Registrar ten weeks before. The minimum period is 14 days before the date of the proposed registration.

After the civil partnership registration you can obtain a copy of the civil partnership certificate from the Registrar on payment of the appropriate fee.

While nothing of a religious nature may be included in the ceremony, it is possible to have music, poetry, exchange of rings, etc. and this should be discussed with the Registrar, as should any flower arrangements. *Refer to the General Register Office (Northern Ireland) website (www.groni.gov.uk) for further information.*

LEGAL PRELIMINARIES

- It is a legal requirement that both parties be of the same sex, aged 18 years or over on the date of application (or able to provide appropriate consent, e.g. from a parent or guardian, if aged 16–18), not be related to each other and not already be in a civil partnership or marriage.

- Notice of intention to form a civil partnership to be given by both parties and you cannot give more than one year's notice. The notice is a legal document that must be given and signed by each of the people forming the partnership.

- You must both have lived in any district in England and Wales for at least seven days immediately before giving notice. However, if one of the partners is subject to immigration control, it will be necessary for both partners to attend a designated register office (see below) to give the required notice. Information on this aspect can be obtained from your local register office. It does not matter if either of you moves to a different address after the notice has been given.

- If you live in different registration districts, you can choose to hold the ceremony in the register office or licensed premise in the district where either of you live or in any register office or licensed premise of your choice. Notice must be given to the Civil Partnership Officer in each district.

- If you both live in the same district, notice must be given by both of you.
  However, it is important to first contact the district where you wish the ceremony to take place.

- Once you have given notice you must wait 15 clear days before the partnership can be formed.

- Partnerships may then be formed between the hours of 8 a.m. and 6 p.m. at any time within 12 months from the day on which you gave notice.

DESIGNATED OFFICE SYSTEM

This relates to a partnership involving someone who is subject to immigration control. Initially a letter must be obtained from the Home Office stating they can form a partnership in the UK. They then need to give formal notice to a Designated Office. Details of such notices will change if one or both of the parties are subject to immigration control and also the location of the persons and their Designated Office. The Home Office or the Superintendent Registrar can supply details and a list of the Designated Offices in England and Wales.

THE NECESSARY DOCUMENTS

When giving notice, you will be asked to produce evidence of identity and nationality – preferably your passport or birth certificate – and proof of residence, e.g. an electricity or telephone bill. With a birth certificate, another form of identification is required – driving licence, medical card, ID card or nationality document stating date of birth.

It is important to note that certain documents will be required if any of the following circumstances apply:
- proof of your parent's or guardian's approval if you are under 18. The relevant form can be obtained from the register office

- evidence if either party has been through a marriage or previous partnership of how your marriage or partnership ended:
  - in the case of divorce, your Decree Absolute bearing an original stamp from the issuing court, with an English translation if appropriate
  - if you have been widowed, the death certificate of your former spouse
  - if you have been in a previous civil partnership, proof of dissolution or annulment of the previous civil formation
- a passport, Home Office Document or other official identity document, with an English translation if appropriate, if born outside the UK
- Deed Poll, Change of Name Deed or Statutory Declaration if you have changed your name.

FEES

Fees are set nationally by Parliament for register office ceremonies held in England and Wales and are regularly reviewed.

A fee will be payable for:
- giving the notices of intent to enter a civil partnership; this is per person in each register office where notice is given
- conducting the partnership registration and one copy of the civil partnership certificate. The fees vary from venue to venue for partnerships in private approved premises. This fee is payable on the day of the ceremony, so be sure to have cash available.

CIVIL PARTNERSHIP IN APPROVED PREMISES

Each local register office holds a list of approved premises in its district. These include banqueting suites, stately homes and other buildings of historical interest.

If you have a civil formation at approved premises, the Civil Partnership Officer will charge a higher fee to take into account the additional administration, time and costs involved in travelling to the venue. The fee will also vary depending on whether the ceremony is to be held on a weekday, Saturday, Sunday or Bank Holiday and is payable in advance. Although these charges are set locally, they tend not to vary significantly from area to area.

The law does not allow for civil formation to be held in the open air, in a tent or marquee, in any other movable structure such as a boat or a hot air balloon, nor in any building that has present or past connection with any religion.

Some venues can only hold the ceremony and you will have to find another venue for the reception. At other venues it is negotiable and some will only allow the ceremony if you have a reception as well. In any case, you should contact the manager or owner of the premises to make provisional arrangements before contacting the register office.

- Notice of intention to form a civil partnership must be given in the district(s) where you both live and the certificate presented to the register office in the district where the ceremony is to be held if they are not the same.

- The same residency rules of seven clear days apply.
- The ceremony may take place at any time within 12 months from the day on which notice was given.

SUGGESTIONS FOR MUSIC, POETRY AND READINGS *(see page 40 of civil ceremony)*

Civil Formation Abroad

Civil partnerships may take place abroad providing the country has existing legislation for such partnerships. You should contact the Consulate/Embassy for the relevant country for advice on what documentation will be required or contact your local register office for further information.

CIVIL PARTNERSHIP CEREMONY – REGISTER OFFICE

The choice of venue is yours as you can hold the ceremony at any register office in England or Wales. Obtain addresses from local authorities, telephone directories or the internet.

Refer to Checklist 6 'Civil Ceremony – Register Office', page 190

❑ Identify the register office of your choice
❑ Telephone the register office to provisionally book the ceremony
This can be arranged up to 12 months in advance

❏ Call in person at the appropriate register office(s) to give notices of your intention to form a civil partnership and to pay the fees for giving notices – *see 'Legal Preliminaries', page 50.* It will be necessary to produce evidence of identity for both parties – *see 'The Necessary Documents', page 52*

❏ Make an appointment with the Civil Partnership Officer to discuss the following details:
- confirm the date and time of ceremony
- how many guests can be accommodated
- type of ceremony – standard or enhanced with the addition of extra non-religious declarations or poetry readings of your choice. The Civil Partnership Officer may be able to offer suggestions if required
- the policy on playing appropriate music of your choice providing it has no religious overtones. The Civil Partnership Officer may be able to offer suggestions if required
- the possibility of including either party or both being 'given away'
- the policy on confetti, photography and video recording
- the possibility of having the ceremony broadcast live on the Internet and the cost
- provision of flowers
  A silk flower arrangement will be provided or you can arrange to supply your own flowers
- location and quantity of parking space for guests' cars
- amount of fees and details of payment

❏ Choose at least two adult witnesses *(this is a legal requirement)*

CIVIL PARTNERSHIP CEREMONY – APPROVED PREMISES

Many stately homes, prestigious buildings, hotels and restaurants – all of which make great backdrops for your photographs – are licensed to hold civil partnership ceremonies. You can obtain details of approved venues from local register offices or on the internet.

Refer to Checklist 7 'Civil Ceremony – Approved Premises', page 192

❏ Decide whether you prefer to have just the ceremony or both the ceremony and reception at the venue
❏ Identify approved venues in the required area *(obtain details from local register office or on the Internet)*
❏ Enquire whether they offer facilities for the ceremony or both the ceremony and reception
❏ Establish compatibility of venue with proposed style of ceremony
❏ Request brochures and prices
❏ Ascertain their hire charges for the room(s) and whether they offer exclusive use of the venue and the cost
❏ Establish availability
  • date
  • time

- room(s) *(depending on the number of guests)*
- ❑ Choose at least two adult witnesses *(this is a legal requirement)*

Booking the Civil Partnership Officer

- ❑ Telephone the register office to provisionally book the Civil Partnership Officer
  This can be arranged up to 12 months in advance
- ❑ Call in person at the appropriate register office(s) to give notices of your intention to form a civil partnership and to pay the fees for giving notices – *see 'Legal Preliminaries', page 50.* It will be necessary to produce evidence of identity for both parties – *see 'The Necessary Documents', page 52*
- ❑ Make an appointment with the Civil Partnership Officer to discuss the following details:
  - confirm the date and time of ceremony
  - proposed venue
  - number of guests attending
  - type of ceremony – standard or enhanced with the addition of extra non-religious declarations or poetry readings of your choice. The Civil Partnership Officer may be able to offer suggestions if required
  - the policy on playing appropriate music of your choice providing it has no religious overtones. The Civil Partnership Officer may be able to offer suggestions if required
  - the possibility of including either party or both being 'given away'

- the policy on confetti, photography and video recording
- amount of fees and details of payment

Booking a venue for the Ceremony only

❑ Make an appointment with the Venue Manager to discuss your requirements:
  - confirm the date and time of ceremony
  - number of guests attending
  - ask whether there are any weddings or other civil formations on the same day
  - check on easy access for any elderly or disabled guests
  - provision of flowers
    Specify the type and colour if you wish the venue to provide them or you may prefer to ask your own florist
  - the policy on confetti
  - location and quantity of parking space for guests' cars
  - discuss the estimated cost and ascertain whether VAT is included
  - request a detailed estimate in writing
❑ Confirm acceptance in writing and enclose the required deposit
❑ One week before the ceremony
  - telephone or call round to check the final arrangements
  - confirm the final number of guests

Booking a venue for the Ceremony and Reception

❑ See 'Booking a venue for the Ceremony only' above
❑ Refer to 'Reception', page 123

MARRYING ABROAD

It is becoming increasingly popular to combine the wedding and honeymoon in an exotic location. The legal requirements and procedures for marriage differ from one country to another. It is, therefore, important to establish exactly what is required for your intended location. Many leading tour operators offer a comprehensive wedding package and have a Wedding Department to assist you with all the necessary arrangements. They will request a minimum of 10 weeks to process all the paperwork.

Civil partnerships may take place abroad providing the country has existing legislation for such partnerships. You should contact the Consulate/Embassy for the relevant country for advice on what documentation will be required or contact your local register office for further information.

Refer to Checklist 8 'Marrying Abroad', page 195

❑ Decide if it is appropriate to consult a Superintendent Registrar – *see 'Marrying Abroad', page 41*
❑ Decide how you wish to book your wedding – *see 'Honeymoon', page 162*
  • holiday company • travel agent • website
❑ Set a provisional budget

❑ Discuss whether you will get married and take your
honeymoon at the same destination or different ones
❑ Identify suitable destinations
❑ Establish the required period of residency before the
ceremony can take place *Usually 3–5 working days*
❑ Decide on length of stay *(allow for period of residency and to
complete the legal formalities)*
❑ Decide if you wish to invite any family and friends to attend
the ceremony
❑ Consider whether you wish to have a church Service of
Blessing – *see 'Service of Blessing', page 64*
❑ Discuss your requirements with the tour operator. If they offer
a wedding package, ascertain what is included and the cost:
  • wedding insurance to cover your wedding attire being lost or
    damaged, your photographs needing to be re-taken, etc.
  • transportation costs to the resort authorities
  • Marriage Licence and Certificate
  • services of the Registrar
  • wedding cake
  • hors d'oeuvres
  • sparkling wine or champagne
  • bouquet, buttonhole, additional flowers and decorations
  • musicians
  • photographs and video.

THE NECESSARY DOCUMENTS

All resort authorities require English language documents. If yours are in another language, you should have them officially translated and take the translation with you as well as the original documents. Some countries ask for birth certificates, divorce documents and death certificates to be 'legalised'. This can be done through the Foreign and Commonwealth Office *(the telephone number is listed in your local telephone directory or refer to the website www.fco.gov.uk).*

You will need to ascertain from the tour operator which of the following you require for your chosen location:

- passports
- birth certificates
- Decree Absolute if divorced
- death certificate if widowed
- proof of change of name by Deed Poll
- parental consent *(depending on your age)*
- adoption certificate
- passport photographs
- photocopies of documents prior to travel
- all original documents to be taken out to resort
- translations of foreign documents to be taken out to resort.

ADDITIONAL REQUIREMENTS

Your tour operator will be able to advise you if any special requirements apply to your chosen destination. These may include obtaining a letter prepared by a Notary Public stating that you are free to be married or obtaining an Affidavit to prove single status.

It is advisable to obtain two copies of the marriage certificate at the time of your marriage.

SERVICE OF BLESSING

A service of blessing is sometimes held after a civil ceremony or following marriage abroad. The Church of England calls this 'An Order for Prayer and Dedication after a Civil Marriage'. It can take place directly after the marriage or on another day, including a Sunday. The service can include hymns, prayers, readings, etc., but there is no exchange of vows.

Refer to Checklist 9 'Service of Blessing', page 197

❑ Make an appointment with the church officiant to discuss the following details:
- date and time of ceremony
- content and order of service – *see 'Order of Service', page 25*
- bell-ringers, organist and choir and the relevant cost
- suggest a meeting with the organist and obtain a contact telephone number
- check if there are any other ceremonies on the same day
- flowers and who will provide them
  Some churches provide flowers and you may wish to state a preference for the type and colour. Ascertain whether you will be required to contribute towards the cost
- permission for photography and video recording
- amount of church fees and details of payment
- date for a rehearsal, if required

❑ Make an appointment with the organist to discuss the music –
 see 'Order of Service', page 25
❑ Make a sketch of the inside of the church if required by the
 photographer, videographer, etc.
❑ Ascertain location and quantity of parking space for guests'
 cars

FLOWERS

There is nothing more beautiful than the sight and smell of flowers in bloom and they will be an essential part of your big day.

From the wedding service to the bride's bouquet, and from the wedding reception to the buttonholes and corsages, wedding flowers are everywhere to be seen. Co-ordinating the 'floral package' so that it complements the day and makes the best use of seasonal flowers requires careful planning and the professional advice of a florist.

Refer to Checklist 10 'Flowers', page 199

❑ Consider provision of flowers for the church or civil ceremony, following discussion with officiant, Superintendent Registrar, Civil Partnership Officer or venue manager – *see 'Church Wedding', page 23, 'Civil Ceremony – Register Office', page 42, 'Civil Ceremony – Approved Premises', page 44, 'Civil Partnership - Register Office'', page 55 or 'Civil Ceremony – Approved Premises, page 57*

❑ Consider provision of flowers for the reception

❑ Choose a florist
- recommendation • good reputation • advertisement
- website

- ask to see photographs and samples of their work or look at online images
☐ Establish their availability on the date you require
☐ Make an appointment to discuss your requirements:
  - show the florist pictures of relevant flower designs that appeal to you
  - outline the colour scheme and style of flowers
  - specify any favourite flowers
  - bouquets headdresses corsages buttonholes
    Take along sketches or photographs of your dress and attendants' clothes and any pieces of fabric, ribbon, etc.
  - flowers for the ceremony
  - flowers for the reception
  - estimated total cost
☐ Book florist
☐ Pay a deposit and discuss payment details
☐ Write to confirm requirements or request confirmation
☐ Specify delivery or collection arrangements, times and venues
☐ Exchange mobile telephone numbers for use on the day

PHOTOGRAPHY

Your wedding photographs are the lasting images of your special day, so be sure you find the right photographer to capture all the magic, the people and special moments in the day.

Refer to Checklist 11 'Photography', page 203

❑ Choose a photographer or photographic studio. *It is suggested you look at three portfolios. A website is an excellent way to view the photographer's images and styles*
  - recommendation   • good reputation   • advertisement
  - website
  - establish their availability on the date you require
  - request brochures and details of charges
❑ Arrange a meeting to discuss your requirements:
  - establish that the photographer you meet will be the one who will be covering your wedding or civil formation
  - request to see their own portfolio of complete weddings, not just their best images
  - discuss fees and cost of photographs, including package deals and any extras you may have to pay for
  - establish whether the cost of an album or digital image CD is included in the package, or just the photographs
  - establish the availability of an online photo album for viewing and ordering

- ascertain when the proofs or online images will be ready and for how long they will be available while you make your selection
- enquire when the prints will be ready
- check how long the negatives or digital images will be retained
- estimated total cost
❏ Book photographer
❏ Pay a deposit and discuss payment details
❏ Arrange a meeting to be held approximately one week before the wedding to discuss the following points:
  - confirm date, times and venues
  - exchange mobile telephone numbers for use on the day
  - discuss options and requirements for informal photographs
  - any special effects, black & white or sepia images required
  - ensure that your photographer knows what formal pictures you require. These might include the following:

Pictures at Home
Portraits of bride
Bride with bridesmaid(s) and pageboy(s)
Bride with parents
Family group(s)

At the Church/Register Office/Approved Premises
Groom
Groom, best man and ushers
Groom and his parents

During the Ceremony *(if permitted)*
Signing the register
With officiant, Registrar or Civil Partnership Officer and witnesses

After the Ceremony
Bride and groom

Groups
Bride, groom and best man
Bride, groom, best man, bridesmaid(s)/pageboy(s) and ushers
Bride and groom with parents
Bride's family group
Groom's family group
Friends
Complete wedding group

At the Reception
Portraits of bride and groom

- delivery or collection of proof album and confirm details of online images
- advise guests about online images with website address and password

VIDEO

A well made wedding video can provide an invaluable lasting memento of the occasion, recording many of the amusing incidents you missed and capturing the planned events, as well as those spontaneous moments that are unique to every wedding.

Refer to Checklist 12 'Video', page 205

❑ Before you proceed with booking a videographer, it is advisable to obtain the permission of the officiant, Superintendent Registrar or Civil Partnership Officer. Ask if there are any restrictions on where you can film in the venue and if more than one camera is allowed *(often one camera is placed at the back of the venue looking up the aisle and another will be adjacent to the couple)*

❑ Decide whether you will ask a friend or use a professional company

❑ If you choose a friend, ensure they have the necessary video camera and equipment, editing facilities and DVD burning equipment or arrange to hire. Ensure they know how to use the equipment and understand how to film a wedding

❑ Choose a videographer. *It is suggested you contact two or three videographers to ensure you choose the most appropriate one to make your video. Check on their professional experience and training*

- recommendation   • good reputation   • advertisement
- website
- request brochures and details of charges
- borrow sample videos. *Ask to see a recent full-length wedding video rather than just a show-reel of the highlights of other weddings*
- establish their availability on the date you require
❑ Make an appointment to discuss your requirements:
  - date, times and venues
  - details of coverage
  - additional sound-track or background music
  - edited highlights
  - copyright clearance for music and songs
  - establish the approximate running time of the finished video
  - estimated number of DVD copies
  - estimated total cost
❑ Book videographer
❑ Pay a deposit and discuss payment details
❑ Write to confirm requirements or request confirmation
❑ Arrange a meeting to be held approximately one week before the wedding
❑ finalise the arrangements
  - confirm date, times and venues
  - exchange mobile telephone numbers for use on the day

If a video of the ceremony is not possible, you may wish to consider the possibility of a sound recording.

❑ Obtain the permission of the officiant, Superintendent Registrar or Civil Partnership Officer and reception venues, as appropriate
❑ Arrange suitable recording equipment and microphone system

TRANSPORT

When deciding on transport, you will need to take into account the style and theme of the wedding and the practical aspects such as distances, journey times and the time of year, especially if you plan to have open-topped transport.

Refer to Checklist 13 'Transport', page 207

❑ Decide on mode of transport
- taxi or mini cab • chauffeur-driven limousine or vintage car
- horse-drawn carriage *(for short distances on quiet roads with no steep hills)*
- riverboat • other

❑ Plan how each member of the bridal party will travel to the ceremony and reception

❑ Ascertain how the groom and best man will travel to the ceremony

❑ Decide how many vehicles you will need to hire or borrow

❑ Check local hire companies for types of vehicles, prices and availability

❑ Make an appointment to view the vehicle(s) and to discuss your requirements:
- date • times • venues
- type, colour and number of vehicles

- • check whether car(s) are being used for other weddings on that day. If so, consider paying extra for exclusive use to ensure punctuality
- • ascertain arrangements for an acceptable substitute in the event of a breakdown or if the vehicle is sold before the wedding
- • proposed uniform of chauffeur, driver or footmen
- • ribbons on the cars or rosettes and plumes for the horses
- • champagne, glasses and an ice bucket
- • estimated total cost

❑ Place booking

❑ Pay a deposit and discuss payment details

❑ Write to confirm requirements or request confirmation

❑ Arrange lifts for guests, if required

❑ Arrange transport to your wedding night venue or to go on honeymoon. If necessary, plan how you will get your own car to the reception

❑ Notify in writing any changes in the plans, e.g. collection address, timings, venues, number of passengers to be transported, additional photo venues

❑ Notify the company of any roadworks, diversions and any special events likely to cause delay that were not known at the time of booking

❑ Exchange mobile telephone numbers for use on the day

INVITATIONS AND GUEST LIST

It is important to check the capacity of the church, register office or approved premises before deciding how many guests to invite to the ceremony and ascertain how many can be catered for at the reception.

❑ Decide how many guests you would like to invite to the ceremony and the reception
❑ Produce a schedule with the suggested columns

Name and Address	Tel.No.	No. of children	Accepted ✓	Refused ✓

❑ Decide how many guests you would like to invite to the evening reception
❑ Produce a schedule with the suggested columns

Name and Address	Tel.No.	No. of children	Accepted ✓	Refused ✓

❑ Decide whether you wish to invite couples with babies or young children
❑ Prepare a guest list for the ceremony and reception and have some names in reserve

❏ Prepare a separate guest list for the evening reception and have some names in reserve

❏ Determine how many invitations are required – *see 'Stationery', page 78*

❏ Decide whether it is appropriate to include any guidance on dress or theme

❏ Decide whether you will include an invitation reply card

❏ Send out the invitations at least six weeks before the wedding and state whether a guest may bring a partner

❏ Record responses as they arrive and send out invitations to people on the reserve list if numbers permit

❏ Acknowledge invitation replies

- send a wedding gift list or information pack *(with reply or on request)*
- enclose a map of the ceremony and reception venues
- include a list of nearby hotels and guesthouses with prices where appropriate
- ask to be notified of any special requirements such as diet, e.g. vegetarian, kosher or allergies, highchairs for babies and wheelchairs for any elderly or disabled guests

STATIONERY

Your wedding invitations are the first glimpse your guests will get of your wedding day, so it's important to make a good first impression. As well as letting them know the all-important details of the day such as date, time and location, your wedding invitations will give them an idea of the tone and theme of your wedding. Choose stationery in complementary colours and styles to match your colour scheme or theme.

Refer to Checklist 14 'Stationery', page 209

Wedding Invitations
❑ Decide whether to write your own or have them printed
❑ Choose a style to suit the wedding *(formal, traditional or modern)*
❑ Size and shape *(rectangular, wedding bell, heart, etc.)*
❑ Background colour   • colour of lettering   • typeface
  • border   • motif
❑ Compose appropriate wording to complement the style of card chosen and decide whether to include a space for your guests' names
❑ Arrange for a proof
  Check spelling, wording, spacing and punctuation with great care
❑ Determine the quantity you will require
  One per couple or family (children over 18 should receive their

*own invitation), officiant, parents, best man, ushers, attendants
and a few spares*
❑ Place the order and confirm the required date of supply

Evening Reception Invitations
❑ Decide whether to write your own or have them printed
❑ Choose a style to complement the wedding invitations
❑ Size and shape *(rectangular, wedding bell, heart, etc.)*
❑ Background colour • colour of lettering • typeface
   • border • motif
❑ Compose appropriate wording
❑ Arrange for a proof
   Check spelling, wording, spacing and punctuation with care
❑ Determine the quantity you will require
❑ Place the order and confirm the required date of supply

Order of Service Sheets
❑ Discuss the order of service with the officiant – *see 'Order of
   Service', page 25*
❑ Decide on a suitable style
❑ Shape and size
❑ Background colour colour of lettering typeface border motif
❑ Arrange for a proof and check carefully
❑ Determine how many you will require
   *One per guest, officiant, organist and each member of the
   choir, plus mementoes*
❑ Place the order and confirm the required date of supply

Miscellaneous

❑ Book matches
❑ Bottleneck labels
❑ Bridal favours
❑ Cake boxes
❑ Candles
❑ Crackers
❑ Drink mats
❑ Guest book
❑ Invitation reply cards
❑ Keepsake album
❑ Menu cards
❑ Paper plates
❑ Party poppers
❑ Personalised celebration balloons
❑ Personalised Holy Bibles *(yourselves, parents, helpers)*
❑ Personalised satin ribbons *(tables, pews, wedding cars)*
❑ Personalised video or DVD cases
❑ Photograph album(s) or digital image CDs
❑ Photograph wallets *(for informal snapshots)*
❑ Place name cards
❑ Serviettes
❑ Serviette rings
❑ Thank-you cards or letters
❑ Wedding sparklers

WEDDING GIFTS

You may wish to consider some wedding gift options. As an alternative to receiving gift items, you could ask guests to pledge gifts to a store operating a bridal account card, contribute towards your honeymoon or request that money be donated to charity.

Stores offering a bridal account card receive pledges and the couple can decide whether they wish to receive the pledged item or buy another item of the same value.

If you decide to have a honeymoon fund, guests may contribute to the overall cost of your trip or pay for specific parts – upgrade to first class travel, activities and excursions. This can be arranged online or co-ordinated by you.

Nowadays couples may opt to ask their guests to donate money to charity rather than buy wedding gifts. Couples register online and choose a charity they wish to support. An online code is given to guests, allowing them to use the website and make a donation.

If you prefer to receive gifts, think about your future lifestyle together and the amount and type of entertaining you will do. Build a picture of the colours and designs you both like and then go through each room listing what you will need. Your list will probably include both practical and decorative items. You may also wish to include tools and equipment for the garden and home improvement.

You should include more items on your list than you expect to receive in order to give people plenty of choice. List some cheaper items as well as some fairly expensive ones that groups of people can purchase together.

You can either arrange your gift list yourself or place it with one or more shops or department stores. In order to avoid duplication, you or the shop should hold a master copy of the list and record details of gifts as they are purchased or promised. Many stores offer an online wedding list service; the convenience and flexibility of this will be of particular benefit to any overseas guests.

Refer to Checklist 15 'Wedding Gifts', page 211

❏ Decide whether you wish to receive gifts, apply for a bridal account card, invite guests to donate to a charity or contribute to your honeymoon fund
❏ Make the necessary arrangements with stores and websites
❏ Prepare the appropriate wedding gift list or information pack
❏ If required, prepare a wedding gift list with the suggested columns

Item	Brand Name	Model/Design/Colour	Size	Qty.	Available from	Cost

❏ Decide whether to place the list with one or more shops or department stores or co-ordinate it yourself

❏ Inform guests when they accept your invitation of your preference and send them the appropriate details of stores and online information.

❏ Keep a record with the suggested columns of gifts or donations as they arrive or are promised

Gift or Donation	Given By/ Promised By	Thank You Sent (date)

❏ Write thank-you letters and note the date on which you sent them

❏ Exchange any damaged or unwanted wedding gifts

GIFTS FOR ATTENDANTS

It is usual for the bride and groom to purchase small gifts for the attendants as a token of appreciation and as a keepsake of the day. These are given to them either at a pre-wedding party or on the morning of the wedding.

- ❏ Purchase gift for the best man
  - credit card holder   • key-ring case   • cigarette lighter
  - pewter tankard   • decanter   • hipflask   • book   • pen
- ❏ Purchase gift for the usher(s)
  - credit card holder   • key-ring case   • cigarette lighter
  - pewter tankard   • calculator   • book   • pen
- ❏ Purchase gift for the bridesmaid(s) and flower girl
  - bracelet   • necklace   • ear-rings   • jewellery box
  - small trinket   • photograph frame   • evening handbag
  - book
- ❏ Purchase gift for the pageboy(s)
  - wristwatch   • calculator   • camera   • framed print
  - computer game   • book   • photograph album
- ❏ Purchase gifts for the witnesses
- ❏ Purchase gifts for any helpers
- ❏ Arrange engraving, if desired
  - wedding date
  - initials
  - personal message

❏ Produce a schedule with the suggested columns

Attendant	Name	Gift	Engraving

DUTIES

DUTIES OF THE BEST MAN

The best man is chosen by the bridegroom and is usually a brother or a good friend. This responsible role involves offering a certain amount of help with the preparations and considerable activity on the wedding day to ensure everything proceeds smoothly and is a complete success.

6 months
❑ Discuss plans with the bride, groom and chief bridesmaid
❑ Help to choose the ushers and explain their duties to them

4 months
❑ Arrange to purchase or hire own clothes and ascertain who will pay – *see 'Clothes for the Bridegroom', page 115, and 'Clothes for the Male Attendants', page 117*
❑ Help the groom and other male attendants to choose their clothes

4 weeks
❑ Organise the stag party
❑ Prepare speech for the reception – *see 'Speeches', page 152*
❑ Visit the ceremony and reception venues with the bride and groom to check on timings, parking arrangements, etc.

1 week

❑ Obtain a list of the family and any guests who are to be personally escorted to their seats and any special seating arrangements at the ceremony

❑ Check the groom has all the necessary documents for the ceremony

❑ Ensure the groom has the travel documents for the honeymoon. If the couple are going abroad, remind him about passports, visas, currency and insurance

❑ Attend the wedding rehearsal *(church only)*

❑ Attend any pre-wedding parties

❑ Liaise with the ushers on the final arrangements

❑ Check for roadworks, diversions and any special events taking place

❑ Arrange transport for the groom and self to the ceremony

❑ Arrange own transport from the reception

❑ Arrange going-away car for the bride and groom

❑ Note details and availability of emergency taxi companies

❑ Finalise speech

❑ Have hair cut

1 day

❑ Collect any hired clothing and accessories

❑ Organise decorations for the going-away car

On the day

❑ Check final arrangements

- ushers • buttonholes • order of service sheets • ring(s)
- any relevant documents for the ceremony • travel documents

❑ Collect telemessages, emails and greetings cards to be read out at the reception

❑ Keep the wedding ring(s) safe until required in the ceremony

❑ Help the groom get ready and make sure he arrives at the venue on time *(at least 20 minutes before the ceremony)*

At the church or civil ceremony

❑ Check on ushers

❑ Ensure any fees are paid to the officiant, Registrar or Civil Partnership Officer, organist, bell-ringers, singers and musicians

❑ Sit in right-hand front row with groom

❑ Produce the ring(s) when requested

❑ Witness the signing of the register, if required

❑ Follow the bride and groom down the aisle, with the chief bridesmaid on your left arm

❑ Assist the photographer in organising guests for the group photographs

❑ Leave for the reception with bridesmaids, following after the bride and groom

At the reception

❑ Stand in the receiving line and greet guests

❑ Announce the speeches and the cutting of the cake, if there is no Master of Ceremonies or Toastmaster

❑ Read out any telemessages, emails and greetings cards
❑ Give the third and final speech, and reply on behalf of the bridesmaids
❑ Dance with the chief bridesmaid once the bride and groom have had the first dance together
❑ Decorate the going-away car
❑ Put luggage in the going-away car
❑ Hand travel documents to the groom
❑ Make sure the couple go and change on time and announce to the guests when they are about to leave
❑ Gather everyone outside to bid the couple farewell
❑ After the couple have departed, be on hand to help out in any way
❑ Take charge of the groom's wedding clothes

After the wedding
❑ Ensure the wedding gifts are safely stored
❑ Return any hired clothing and accessories
❑ Write to the bride and groom to thank them for their gift
❑ Write to the bride's parents to thank them for their hospitality
❑ Write to the groom's parents to thank them for any help and support they offered during the planning stage

DUTIES OF THE CHIEF BRIDESMAID OR MATRON OF HONOUR

The chief bridesmaid is usually a sister or close friend of the bride. She liaises closely with the bride during the wedding preparations and helps with the clothing for any other bridesmaids, flower girl and pageboys. The Matron of Honour is usually the bride's older married sister and is normally the only female attendant.

6 months
❑ Discuss plans with the bride, groom and best man
❑ Discuss dress or outfit with the bride, especially if being made, and ascertain who will pay – *see 'Clothes for the Matron of Honour', page 108, and 'Clothes for the Bridesmaids', page 109*

4 months
❑ Help the bride to choose her dress and the bridesmaids' dresses

4 weeks
❑ Arrange or assist with arrangements for the hen party

1 week
❑ Attend the wedding rehearsal *(church only)*
❑ Attend any pre-wedding parties

1 day
❑ Collect any hired clothing and accessories

On the day
❑ Ensure bouquets are ready for the bride, bridesmaids and flower girl

❑ Help the bride with her hair, make-up and dress
❑ Help the other bridesmaids, flower girl and pageboys get dressed and give them any final instructions on their duties
❑ Leave for the ceremony with the bride's mother 10 minutes before the bride

At the church or civil ceremony
❑ Arrange the bride's dress and veil
❑ Follow behind the bride and her father or giver-away up the aisle
❑ Hold the bride's bouquet during the ceremony
❑ Witness the signing of the register, if required
❑ Leave the church or civil ceremony on the left-hand side of the best man, directly behind the bride and groom
❑ Depart for the reception with the pageboys and any other bridesmaids, after the bride and groom

At the reception
❑ Stand in the receiving line between the groom and the best man to greet guests
❑ Help to display and record gifts received
❑ Have the first dance with the best man
❑ Help the bride to change into her going-away outfit
❑ Hand bouquet to bride when she is about to leave

After the wedding
❑ Return any hired clothing and accessories

❑ Write to the bride and groom to thank them for their gift
❑ Write to the bride's parents to thank them for their hospitality

DUTIES OF THE BRIDESMAIDS

Bridesmaids are usually unmarried sisters or close friends of the bride. Older bridesmaids liaise closely with the bride and chief bridesmaid during the wedding preparations and help with the choice of dresses. Younger ones will not be expected to take an active part in the planning stage and their mothers will get involved instead.

6 months
❑ Discuss plans with the bride, groom, best man and chief bridesmaid
❑ Discuss the bridesmaids' dresses or outfits with the bride, especially if being made, and ascertain who will pay – *see 'Clothes for the Bridesmaids', page 109*

4 months
❑ Help to choose the bridesmaids' dresses

1 week
❑ Attend the wedding rehearsal *(church only)*
❑ Attend any pre-wedding parties, if appropriate

1 day
❑ Collect any hired clothing and accessories, if required

On the day
❏ Receive any final instructions from the chief bridesmaid
❏ Get dressed and help with any younger attendants
❏ Leave for the ceremony with the bride's mother 10 minutes before the bride

At the church or civil ceremony
❏ Follow behind the chief bridesmaid up the aisle
❏ Leave the church or civil ceremony after the chief bridesmaid
❏ Depart for the reception with the chief bridesmaid, any other bridesmaids and pageboys

After the wedding
❏ Return any hired clothing and accessories, if required
❏ Write to the bride and groom to thank them for their gift
❏ Write to the bride's parents to thank them for their hospitality

DUTIES OF THE FLOWER GIRL AND PAGEBOYS

Flower girls and pageboys are usually nieces and nephews or young brothers and sisters and are generally no younger than about five nor older than nine or 10. Flower girls walk in front of the bride carrying posies of flowers or bunches of thornless roses, which they can pass out to the guests as they go. They can also scatter rose or other flower petals before the bride as she walks down the aisle.

Pageboys traditionally carry the bride's train if she is wearing a dress with a long train.

6 months
❑ Bride and respective mothers to discuss clothes and accessories, especially if being made, and ascertain who will pay – *see 'Clothes for the Flower Girl', page 111, and 'Clothes for the Pageboys', page 112*

4 months
❑ Clothes and accessories to be purchased or hired, as appropriate

1 week
❑ Attend the wedding rehearsal *(church only)*
❑ Attend any pre-wedding parties, if appropriate

On the day
❑ Receive any final instructions from the chief bridesmaid
❑ Leave for the ceremony with the bridesmaids 10 minutes before the bride

At the church or civil ceremony
❑ Follow behind the bridesmaids up the aisle
❑ Stand or sit during the ceremony, as instructed
❑ Leave the church or civil ceremony after the bridesmaids
❑ Pose for photographs

❑ Depart for the reception with the bridesmaids

After the wedding

❑ Return of any hired clothing and accessories to be arranged by the respective mothers, if appropriate

❑ Write to the bride and groom to thank them for their gift *(if very young, their parents should write on their behalf)*

❑ Write to the bride's parents to thank them for their hospitality *(if very young, their parents should write on their behalf)*

DUTIES OF THE USHERS

A small wedding does not require ushers. As a general rule, you will need one usher per 50 guests. The ushers are chosen by the groom and his best man and are usually brothers, close relatives or friends of the bride and groom. It is advisable to appoint a chief usher who will direct the others and his specific responsibilities are shown as (CU). Traditionally, the ushers are the responsibility of the best man who ensures they know their duties.

4 months

❑ Arrange to purchase or hire clothes, based on guidance from the bridegroom and best man, and ascertain who will pay – *see 'Clothes for the Bridegroom', page 113, and 'Clothes for the Male Attendants', page 115*

1 week

❑ Confirm final arrangements with the best man and any other

ushers, including time of arrival at the church or civil
ceremony
❏ Obtain from the best man a list of the family and any guests
who are to be personally escorted to their seats and any
special seating arrangements at the ceremony (CU)
❏ Attend the wedding rehearsal, if required *(church only)*
❏ Attend any pre-wedding parties
❏ Obtain a large umbrella
❏ Have hair cut

1 day
❏ Collect any hired clothing and accessories

On the day
❏ Collect buttonholes and order of service sheets from the
bride's home (CU)
❏ Have a large umbrella available if it is likely to rain
❏ Arrive at the venue at least 20 minutes before the ceremony

At the church or civil ceremony
❏ Assist guests with parking if requested
❏ Greet guests as they arrive
  • hand out order of service sheets, hymn and prayer books
  (church only)
  • hand out buttonholes and a corsage to the groom's mother
  • hand out maps showing the route to the reception or give
  directions

❏ Ensure the officiant has order of service sheets for the bride and groom (CU) *(church only)*
❏ Escort the bride's mother and guests to their seats
It is usual for the bride's family and friends to sit on the left and the groom's family and friends on the right. If there is a great imbalance in numbers, the ushers may tactfully ask guests to fill the seating evenly
❏ Endeavour to seat couples with young babies and children near the exit
❏ Escort latecomers to seats at the back of the church or room
❏ In the event of rain, use an umbrella to protect the bride and groom, attendants and immediate family
❏ Assist the best man with organising guests for the group photographs
❏ Direct guests regarding the throwing of confetti
❏ Ensure the church or room is left tidy and collect any property left behind and unused order of service sheets
❏ Ensure guests have transport to the reception

At the reception
❏ Assist guests with parking
❏ Look after any elderly or infirm guests

After the wedding
❏ Return any hired clothes and accessories for self and other male attendants, if required
❏ Write to the bride and groom to thank them for their gift

❑ Write to the bride's parents to thank them for their hospitality

DUTIES OF THE BRIDE'S FATHER OR GIVER-AWAY

The bride's father escorts the bride to the church and gives her away. By prior arrangement with the Superintendent Registrar, it is possible to include the bride being 'given away' in a civil ceremony also. Although this is usually undertaken by the bride's father, a brother, male guardian or uncle may perform this task.

4 months
❑ Arrange to purchase or hire clothes and ascertain who will pay – *see 'Clothes for the Bridegroom', page 113, and 'Clothes for the Male Attendants', page 115*

4 weeks
❑ Ask the officiant to say grace if he is attending the reception
❑ Prepare speech for the reception, and grace, if necessary – *see 'Speeches', page 152*

1 week
❑ Attend the wedding rehearsal *(church only)*
❑ Attend any pre-wedding parties
❑ Finalise speech
❑ Have hair cut

1 day
❏ Collect any hired clothing and accessories

On the day
❏ Escort the bride from home to the church or civil ceremony

At the church
❏ Arrive last with the bride
❏ Lead procession up the aisle, walking on the bride's right-hand side
❏ Offer the bride's right hand to the officiant at the appropriate time
❏ Give away the bride
❏ Stand until after the vows, and then join bride's mother in the front pew
❏ Accompany the bride's mother to the vestry for the signing of the register
❏ Sign the register and escort the bride's mother down the aisle
❏ Leave for the reception immediately after the bride and groom

At the civil ceremony
❏ Arrive last with the bride
❏ Lead procession up the aisle, walking on the bride's right-hand side
❏ Give away the bride

❏ Stand until after the vows, and then join bride's mother in the front row of seats

❏ Accompany the bride's mother for the signing of the register

❏ Sign the register and escort the bride's mother out of the room

❏ Leave for the reception immediately after the bride and groom

At the reception

❏ Stand in second place in the receiving line, after the bride's mother, and greet the guests

❏ Say grace if the officiant is not present

❏ Propose a toast to the bride and groom and make the first speech

❏ Mix among guests and introduce them

After the wedding

❏ Return any hired clothing and accessories

DUTIES OF THE BRIDE'S MOTHER

The bride's mother may have a key role in helping with many of the arrangements, but these days more couples are opting to participate significantly in the preparations or may even wish to undertake all the tasks themselves. However, as a matter of courtesy, she can expect to be kept up-to-date with the progress of the preparations.

The wording in italics indicates tasks that may be performed by the bride's mother, if required.

6 months
- ❑ Discuss the plans with the bride, groom and the groom's parents
- ❑ Arrange the reception and entertainment – *see 'Reception', page 123*
- ❑ Assist the bride to plan her wedding dress and the outfits to be worn by the attendants – *see 'Clothes for the Bride', page 104, and 'Clothes for the Bridesmaids, Flower Girl and Pageboys', pages 109–112*
- ❑ Arrange flowers – *see 'Flowers', page 66*
- ❑ Book a photographer – *see 'Photography', page 68*
- ❑ Book a videographer – *see 'Video', page 71*
- ❑ Arrange transport – *see 'Transport', page 74*
- ❑ Compile the guest list – *see 'Invitations and Guest List', page 76*
- ❑ Keep the groom's parents informed of progress

5 months
- ❑ *Organise stationery – see 'Stationery', page 78*

4 months
- ❑ Arrange outfit and accessories, conferring with the groom's mother regarding colour and style

3 months
❑ *Arrange the wedding cake and delivery to the reception venue – see 'Wedding Cake', page 149*
❑ *Help with the wedding gift list and receive the presents as they arrive – see 'Wedding Gifts', page 81*

2 months
❑ *Send out invitations and keep a record of the replies*

4 weeks
❑ *Arrange press announcements*
❑ *Co-ordinate overnight accommodation for guests, if required – see 'Accommodation and Hospitality', page 159*

1 week
❑ Attend the wedding rehearsal *(church only)*
❑ Attend any pre-wedding parties

1 day
❑ Display wedding gifts if the reception is at home

On the day
❑ Help the bride with her dress and veil
❑ Carry a comb, mirror, handkerchief, etc. for use by the bride and attendants – *see 'Hair and Beauty', page 117*
❑ Travel to the ceremony with the bridesmaids and pageboys, 10 minutes before the bride

❑ Escorted by an usher, take a seat in the front left row
❑ Accompany the bride's father for the signing of the register
❑ Sign the register and walk down the aisle on the left arm of
   the bride's father, following the bridesmaids and pageboys
❑ Leave for the reception with the other parents

At the reception
❑ Stand in first place in the receiving line and greet guests with
   the bride's father
❑ Act as hostess, mixing with the guests and introducing them
❑ Help the bride to change into her going-away outfit and take
   care of her dress and accessories, if required

After the wedding
❑ Direct the clearing-up operation if the reception is at home
❑ Take care of the bride's dress and accessories
❑ Send pieces of cake and/or an order of service sheet to
   people who could not attend the wedding – *see 'After the
   Wedding', page 165*
❑ Organise photograph proofs and collect orders – *see 'After the
   Wedding', page 165*
❑ Pass photograph orders to the photographer – *see 'After the
   Wedding', page 165*
❑ Collect and distribute photographs – *see 'After the Wedding',
   page 165*

CLOTHES

CLOTHES FOR THE BRIDE

Your dress will be an important focal point of the day whether you have a church or civil wedding, and you will want to feel confident and radiant. A formal, long dress is equally suitable for a church or civil ceremony, although many brides prefer to wear a suit or short dress for a civil wedding. Allow yourself plenty of time to make decisions and for the dress to be completely ready for the wedding day.

Refer to Checklist 16 'Clothes for the Bride', page 213

❑ Set a provisional budget
❑ Discuss your plans with the groom to ensure colour and style co-ordination between yourselves and your respective attendants
❑ Choose the colour scheme for your dress and your attendants' outfits
❑ Decide whether you will buy, hire or have your dress made
❑ Choose the style, taking into account your personality, proportions, height and figure *(accentuate your good points and minimise the rest)*
  • modern • formal • period, e.g. Victorian, Edwardian, Twenties
  • length and shape of dress

- sleeves *(depending on the time of year)*
- trimmings and decoration
- train *(it is advisable to have a detachable train so it can be removed for the reception and any dancing, unless you intend to change into a different outfit after the ceremony)*
- fabric *(depending on the time of year)*

Having Your Dress Made

❏ Identify a reputable dressmaker
  - personal experience   • recommendation   • advertisement
  - website
❏ Arrange a meeting to discuss your ideas
❏ Decide whether to buy a pattern or have a pattern made from a sketch or picture
❏ Agree a provisional timetable for fittings and completion
❏ Discuss the estimated total cost
❏ Purchase the fabric and any trimmings

Buying or Hiring Your Dress

❏ Allow plenty of time and avoid peak shopping hours
❏ Take someone with you whose opinions and judgement you trust
❏ Try on lots of different styles and look at yourself in the mirror from all angles, particularly the back, which will be most visible to the congregation during the ceremony
❏ Check whether there is a charge for cleaning and alterations

Headddress

❑ Decide whether to wear it on its own or with a veil
❑ Choose an appropriate style to complement your dress and
   any decorative features, and to suit your proposed hairstyle for
   the wedding day
   • tiara • head-hugging Juliet cap • circlet of fresh or silk
     flowers • a single bloom • cluster of flowers • ribbons
     trimmed with flowers • hat *(some styles of dresses, e.g.
     Edwardian, may look better with a hat, perhaps trimmed with
     flowers or feathers)*

Veil

❑ Consider how it will be fixed and how well it will stay in place
❑ Colour
❑ Choose a length to suit your dress
   The more formal your dress, the longer the veil
❑ Choose a style to complement your dress
   • plain • patterned • plain or decorative edging

Accessories

❑ Shoes
   *Colour to match or tone with your dress. It is possible to have
   plain white satin shoes dyed. Comfortable, non-slip, with size
   of heel to complement the style of dress and your height*

❑ Underwear
- bra
  Well-fitting, cream, flesh pink or peach colour, and in a plain style to avoid colour and trimmings showing through your dress
- pants
  Comfortable and ultrasmooth, especially if dress is tight-fitting
- petticoat

❑ Stockings or tights
Stockings are cool and glamorous; tights are warmer and more comfortable. Take into account the fit of your dress. Plain or patterned with bows or hearts. Have a spare pair available

❑ Gloves

❑ Jewellery

❑ Parasol • fan • white prayer book • bible • pomander
You could consider holding one of the above instead of a bouquet

Something old
Something new
Something borrowed
Something blue

Going-away Outfit
❑ Discuss with the groom what he intends to wear for going-away

❑ Choose an outfit that you can wear on other occasions
❑ Choose style and fabric for the time of year and also taking into account the location and climate of your next destination
❑ Purchase appropriate accessories
  • hat • shoes • handbag • gloves • tights

CLOTHES FOR THE MATRON OF HONOUR

Traditionally, the bride's parents pay for the bride's attendants' dresses. However, increasingly these days, more attendants are offering to pay for their own clothes, especially if they can be worn again after the wedding.

Refer to Checklist 17 'Clothes for the Matron of Honour', page 216

❑ Liaise with the Matron of Honour to ensure colour and style co-ordination
❑ Discuss whether her outfit will be purchased, hired or specially made and who will pay
❑ Agree a suitable style, taking into account her personality, proportions, height and figure *(accentuate her good points and minimise the rest)*
  • length and shape of dress or outfit
  • sleeves *(depending on the time of year)*
  • trimmings and decoration
  • fabric *(depending on the time of year)*
❑ Agree on the colour, taking into account the colour of her hair and complexion

Headdress

❏ Choose an appropriate style to complement her dress and any decorative features, and to suit her proposed hairstyle on the wedding day
  - circlet of fresh or silk flowers   • a single bloom   • cluster of flowers   • ribbons trimmed with flowers   • a hat

Accessories

❏ Ascertain what accessories she already owns, which ones will need to be purchased or hired and who will pay
  - shoes
    Colour to match or tone with her dress. It is possible to have plain white satin shoes dyed. Comfortable, non-slip, with size of heel to complement the style of her dress and her height
  - stockings or tights
  - jewellery

CLOTHES FOR THE BRIDESMAIDS

Allow plenty of time for clothes to be made to take account of late fittings and any adjustments, particularly if any young bridesmaids are still growing. Younger bridesmaids may not take a very active part in decision-making and their mothers will get involved instead.

Refer to Checklist 18 'Clothes for the Bridesmaids', page 218

❏ Liaise with the bridesmaids and/or their mothers to ensure colour and style co-ordination

❏ Discuss whether their outfits will be purchased, hired or specially made and who will pay

❏ Agree a suitable style, taking into account the personality, proportions, height and figure of each one *(accentuate good points and minimise the rest)*
  - length and shape of dress
  - sleeves *(depending on the time of year)*
  - trimmings and decoration
  - fabric *(depending on the time of year)*

❏ Agree on the colour, taking into account the colour of hair and complexion of each bridesmaid

Headdress

❏ Choose an appropriate style to complement the dresses and any decorative features, and to suit the proposed hairstyle of each bridesmaid on the wedding day
  - circlet of fresh or silk flowers   • a single bloom   • cluster of flowers   • ribbons trimmed with flowers   • a hat

Accessories

❏ Ascertain what accessories each one already owns, which ones will need to be purchased or hired and who will pay

- shoes

  Colour to match or tone with the dresses. It is possible to have plain white satin shoes dyed. Comfortable, non-slip, with size of heels to complement the style of dresses and height of each bridesmaid
- petticoat
- stockings or tights
- jewellery

CLOTHES FOR THE FLOWER GIRL

The flower girl is usually very young and her mother will get involved in the decision-making. It may be advisable not to have her dress made too early, as late alterations will almost certainly be necessary to take account of her growing. The style and colour of dress should be distinct from the bridesmaids, but should complement the dresses worn by the bride and bridesmaids.

Refer to Checklist 19 'Clothes for the Flower Girl', page 220

❑ Liaise with the flower girl's mother to ensure colour and style co-ordination

❑ Discuss whether her dress will be purchased, hired or specially made and who will pay

❑ Agree a suitable style
- length and shape of dress *(mid-calf length is advisable to prevent her tripping over)*
- sleeves *(depending on the time of year)*
- trimmings and decoration

- fabric *(depending on the time of year)*
❑ Agree on the colour, taking into account the colour of her hair and complexion

Headdress

❑ Choose an appropriate style to complement her dress and any decorative features, and to suit her proposed hairstyle for the wedding day
  - circlet of fresh or silk flowers • a single bloom • cluster of flowers • ribbons trimmed with flowers

Accessories

❑ Ascertain what accessories she already owns, which ones will need to be purchased or hired and who will pay
  - shoes
    Black patent or colour to match or tone with her dress. Comfortable and non-slip
  - petticoat
  - socks or tights
  - jewellery

CLOTHES FOR THE PAGEBOYS

Traditional outfits for small boys include a miniature sailor's uniform, a kilt and sporran, velvet pantaloons and waistcoat, with a full-sleeved shirt underneath, or a military uniform if the groom is an officer and is wearing uniform. Older boys could wear the same type of clothes as the groom and male attendants.

If the pageboys are very young, their mothers will get involved in the decision-making. It may be advisable not to arrange to hire or have their outfits made too early, as late alterations will almost certainly be necessary to take account of them growing.

Refer to Checklist 20 'Clothes for the Pageboys', page 222

❑ Liaise with them or their mothers to ensure colour and style co-ordination with the bridegroom and bridesmaids
❑ Decide whether their outfits will be purchased, hired or specially made and who will pay
❑ Agree a suitable colour and style of outfit

Accessories
❑ Decide what accessories they will wear. Ascertain what they already own, which ones will need to be purchased or hired and who will pay
  • shoes
    Shoes should be comfortable and non-slip
  • tie/cravat
  • cufflinks/tie pin

CLOTHES FOR THE BRIDEGROOM

Discuss your ideas with the bride to ensure colour and style co-ordination between yourselves and your respective attendants.

Decide whether it will be appropriate for you to wear a lounge suit (informal) or morning dress (formal). It is important that you feel comfortable and wear an outfit that is well fitting and suitable for the style of wedding.

Refer to Checklist 21 'Clothes for the Bridegroom', page 224

❑ Decide whether you will buy off the peg, hire or have made-to-measure

❑ Ensure that the best man, bride's father and ushers wear outfits that co-ordinate in style and colour with your own

Accessories

❑ Decide what accessories you will wear. Consider which items you already own and which ones you will either buy or hire
- waistcoat
- shirt
- hat
- gloves
- shoes
- socks
- tie/cravat
- cufflinks/tie pin
- wristwatch

Going-away Outfit

❑ Discuss your ideas with the bride to ensure colour and style co-ordination

❑ Choose style and fabric for the time of the year and also taking into account the location and climate of your next destination
❑ Decide whether to buy a new outfit
❑ Ensure you have the appropriate accessories
  • shirt
  • tie
  • shoes
  • socks

CLOTHES FOR THE MALE ATTENDANTS

Liaise with the best man, bride's father and ushers to ensure colour and style co-ordination. It is important that they feel comfortable and wear an outfit that is well fitting and compatible with what the bridegroom will be wearing.

Refer to Checklist 22 'Clothes for the Male Attendants', page 226

❑ Decide whether their outfits will be hired or purchased and who will pay

Accessories
❑ Decide what accessories they will wear. Ascertain which items they already own, which ones will need to be purchased or hired and who will pay
  • waistcoat
  • shirt
  • hat

- gloves
- shoes
- socks
- tie/cravat
- cufflinks/tie pin
- wristwatch

HAIR AND BEAUTY

Your wedding day is the most important day of your life and you will want to feel and look wonderful. Perhaps you've set yourself a weight loss goal or maybe your wedding is simply the catalyst for a bit of self-improvement and pampering.

Refer to Checklist 23 'Hair and Beauty', page 228

6 months

❏ Weight

If you want to lose a few pounds, now is the time to begin. Concentrate on a routine of healthy eating rather than a crash diet

❏ Diet

Eating a healthy, varied diet rich in anti-oxidants, such as fruits and vegetables, will benefit all aspects of your health and beauty. It is important to drink plenty of water (6–8 glasses per day) in order to improve the appearance and texture of your skin and to enhance the body's cleansing process

❏ Exercise

Try to take some extra exercise, such as walking, swimming or cycling. It will make you feel healthier and more relaxed, increase your circulation and will speed up the rate of metabolism if you are trying to shed any excess weight

❏ Health Spa or Beauty Salon

Spend a few days at a health spa if your budget permits. Expert advice, beauty therapies, sports and exercise facilities are all available to make you feel pampered and come away feeling like a million dollars. Check on what is included in the price and the cost of optional extras. Alternatively, contact your local beauty salon to put together a programme of treatments

❏ Skin Care

Have a consultation at a beauty salon to discuss any skin problems. A skin care therapist will recommend a home care regime and put together a treatment plan. Treat yourself to some good quality skin care preparations. Regular cleansing, toning and moisturising will ensure your skin stays healthy and free from blemishes

❏ Hands and Nails

Your hands will be the focus of attention when you show off your wedding ring. Take extra care shaping your nails and avoid doing things that may cause them to split or break. Wear rubber gloves and use lots of hand cream. If your budget allows, book monthly manicures or purchase some professional hand and nail care products to use on a regular basis at home

3 months

❏ Make-up

Identify a make-up artist if required and have a practice session

❑ De-tox

Due to the effects of de-tox programmes, they are better started months rather than weeks before your wedding day

2 months

❑ Make-up

Arrange a make-up lesson or pick up a few tips from a cosmetic house beautician in a large store. Wear something in the colour of your dress or drape a towel or piece of fabric to get the effect. If you are doing your own make-up, buy any new cosmetics and start practising your wedding day look. You may also wish to buy a matching nail varnish. When purchasing make-up, remember to consider the difference in skin tone if you are planning a fake tan application prior to the wedding

❑ Beauty Treatments

List any treatments you may require – facial, exfoliation, waxing (full leg, half leg, underarm, bikini line), manicure, pedicure, massage, Botox, eyelash/eyebrow tinting and eyebrow shaping. Decide whether to go to a salon, have a beautician come to your home or do them yourself. Make appointments well in advance to avoid disappointment and to ensure you can book the most convenient times

❑ Hair

Make an appointment with your hairdresser to discuss your wedding day hairstyle, especially if you plan to have a new style or wish to adapt it for going away. Take your veil or headdress, if possible. Discuss plans if you intend to cut, curl or colour your hair, or have hair extensions, and make the necessary appointments. Decide whether you will visit the salon on the wedding day or ask your hairdresser to come to your home. Make an appointment or agree the time and place

1 month

❑ Facial

Allow time for any spots, caused by impurities being drawn to the surface, to heal

❑ Tanning

If you wish to have a fake tan that will look flattering in the photographs and video, it is advisable to have a trial spray tanning session to ensure you are happy with the result and colour

1 week

❑ Hair

Attend appointment for cut, curl, colour and hair extensions, as required. Take along veil or headdress and have a final rehearsal. Practise with your hair and headdress if you are doing your own hair on the wedding day

❑ Beauty Treatments

Attend appointments for waxing (full leg, half leg, underarm, bikini line), exfoliation, eyelash/eyebrow tinting and eyebrow shaping. Enjoy being pampered and feel your confidence growing

❏ Sauna
   A sauna or steam bath will leave you feeling refreshed and the
   steam will draw any impurities to the surface of the skin
❏ Massage
   Relax and let go of any tension

2/3 days
❏ Check eyebrow shaping
❏ Tanning
❏ Go along for your final session of spray tanning

1 day
❏ Manicure and pedicure
❏ Assemble beauty preparations and make-up for the
   honeymoon, including sunscreen and after-sun lotion
❏ Assemble a touch-up kit for the wedding day – lipstick,
   blusher, powder, perfume, comb, mirror, tissues and safety
   pins. Your mother should have this available for you
❏ Relax and have an early night

On the day
❏ Have a warm bath or shower
❏ Breakfast
   Eat as substantial a breakfast as you can
❏ Hair
❏ Make-up
❏ Carry out any last minute repairs to nails

❏ Give your touch-up kit to your mother
❏ Get dressed and fix veil or headdress
❏ Take a few deep breaths and enjoy the day

RECEPTION

Once all the formalities of the ceremony are over, the reception is your time to relax with your guests. Ideally, it should reflect the overall style or theme of your wedding. The two biggest decisions you will make when planning your wedding reception will involve the venue and the food and drink.

❑ Decide how many people will attend
  - bridal party • attendants • officiant guests
❑ Decide whether it will be formal or informal
❑ Consider whether you intend to have an evening reception
❑ Decide on an appropriate venue
  - hotel • restaurant • banqueting room • hall or function room • at home • other *(riverboat, canal barge, etc.)*
  Take the following into account:
  - number of guests
  - budget *(set a maximum cost per head)*
  - theme
  - proximity of venue where the ceremony is being held
  - time of day
  - type of food *(sit down meal, fork or finger buffet, barbecue)*
  - licence to consume alcohol
  - provision of entertainment

HOTEL, RESTAURANT OR BANQUETING ROOM

This type of venue offers a one-stop solution to all your requirements – catering, service and facilities – thus reducing the amount of organisation that is required.

Refer to Checklist 24 'Reception – Hotel, Restaurant, Banqueting Room', page 231

How to Choose a Venue

❏ Identify several suitable ones
  - personal experience   - recommendation   - reputation
  - advertisement
❏ Establish their availability on the date you require
❏ Request brochures, sample menus and prices
❏ Dine at one or two of them, if possible, looking at these points:
  - decor
  - atmosphere *(formal or relaxed)*
  - standard of food and service
  - efficiency and friendliness of staff
  - value for money
❏ Determine what size room(s) you require
❏ Establish what bar facilities are available
❏ Ascertain the availability and quantity of car parking space
❏ Telephone the banqueting or restaurant manager to confirm availability
  - date
  - time

- room(s) *(depending on style of reception and number of guests)*
☐ Arrange a meeting with the banqueting or restaurant manager to discuss your requirements.

Number of Guests
- Reception   • evening reception
- Ascertain when the final numbers are required
- Enquire whether they offer a wedding package and, if so, what it includes

Hire Charges
- Discuss any hire charges for the room(s)
- Check whether there are any other weddings on the same day
- Enquire whether there is a charge for exclusive use of the venue, if required

Times
- Ascertain whether there will be any time restrictions
- Discuss the timings:
    - arrival
    - meal
    - speeches
    - cutting the cake
    - evening reception
    - buffet
    - entertainment

- bar closes
- finish

Facilities

- Discuss seating arrangements, room layout and position of the cake table
- Determine whether an evening reception will necessitate a different room layout
- Discuss arrangements for decorating the room (balloons, etc.)
- Discuss arrangements if you wish to display your wedding gifts
- Ask whether they can be kept in a safe place before and after the reception
- Advise your delivery and collection arrangements for the gifts
- Enquire about the provision of a marquee, if required – *see 'Marquees', page 137*
- Ask whether a public address system is available for the speeches
- Enquire whether a changing room is available
- Check on cloakroom facilities
- Check whether there is adequate car parking space
- Ascertain whether a room could be available for children to have a rest or as a quiet room
- Check access for any elderly or disabled guests
- Check they have insurance cover for public liability
- Check on availability of overnight accommodation
  - yourselves • guests
- Enquire whether there is a special rate for accommodation

Flowers

- Discuss whether they will provide the flowers or you will supply your own
- Specify type and colour of flowers, if necessary
- Discuss where the flowers will be placed

Food

- Decide on the provision of canapés or nibbles on arrival
- Finger buffet • fork buffet • sit-down meal • barbecue
- Discuss the menus
  - • reception • evening reception
- Select from the set menus or make your own suggestions
- Advise any special dietary requirements, e.g. kosher, vegetarian or allergies
- Request special menu or small portions for children
- Confirm when the wedding cake will arrive and any special serving instructions

Drinks

- Specify drinks to be served on arrival *(champagne, buck's fizz, sherry, fruit juice, etc.)*
- Select wine – ask if corkage is charged if you are permitted to provide your own wine
- Soft drinks, fruit juice and mineral water
- Champagne or sparkling wine served with the cake

- Liqueurs, brandy, port served with the coffee
- Specify when you would like drinks to be served and in what quantity
- Bar facilities – specify provision of free drinks or pay bar

Staff

- Establish the proposed number of serving and bar staff to be provided
- Ascertain whether they can arrange a Master of Ceremonies or Toastmaster, if required *(the Duty Manager may be able to perform this task)*
- Discuss handing out of bridal favours, e.g. sugared almonds
- Check whether they provide cloakroom staff

Equipment

- State preferred colour of the tablecloths and napkins
- Request candelabra and specify the colour of the candles, if required
- Enquire whether they can provide a cake-stand and knife

Entertainment

- Establish whether entertainment is permitted
- If so, discuss your plans for a disco, live band, entertainment – *see 'Entertainment', page 157*
- Check on lighting, power supply and changing facilities
- Discuss background music or musicians playing during the meal, if required

- Consider providing entertainment for any children, e.g. a clown, magician, puppet theatre or a video, and the availability of a room

Confirmation
- Discuss the estimated cost and ascertain whether VAT and service charge have been included in the prices
- Request a detailed estimate in writing
- Confirm acceptance in writing and enclose the required deposit

Overnight Accommodation
- Reserve rooms, as appropriate
  - yourselves   • guests

One week before
- Telephone or call round to check the final arrangements
- Confirm final numbers
- Provide seating plan and place name cards

HALL OR FUNCTION ROOM

Hiring a hall or function room will allow you more space and flexibility than holding the reception at home, whilst giving you plenty of scope to add your own personal touches. It provides the opportunity to self-cater or use professional caterers and is generally less costly than a hotel.

Refer to Checklist 25 'Reception – Hall or Function Room', page 234

How to Choose a Hall or Function Room

❑ Decide what size room(s) you require, depending on the style of reception and number of guests

❑ Identify several suitable venues

- personal experience • recommendation • advertisement
- website

❑ Establish their availability on the date you require

❑ Enquire about the basic cost and size of room

❑ Arrange to visit them looking for these points:

- decor
- kitchen facilities *(you may need to consider the feasibility of hiring a mobile kitchen)*
- cloakroom and toilet facilities
- availability of car parking space

❑ Confirm availability with the manager:

- date
- time
- room(s)

❑ Arrange a meeting with the manager to discuss your requirements.

Number of Guests

- Reception
- Evening reception
- Ascertain when the final numbers are required

- Enquire whether a wedding package is available and, if so, what it includes

Hire Charges
- Discuss hire charges for the room(s)
- Check whether there are any other weddings on the same day
- Enquire whether there is a charge for exclusive use of the venue

Times
- Ascertain whether there will be any time restrictions
- Discuss the timings:
  - access for decoration and preparation
  - access for caterers
  - arrival of guests
  - evening reception
  - entertainment
  - bar closes
  - finish
  - access for clearing away

Food and Drink
- Advise type of food to be served
- Advise the manager of your catering arrangements *(professional or self-catering)*
- Check the rules regarding the consumption of alcohol
- Discuss bar facilities *(free drinks or a pay bar)*

Facilities

- Discuss seating arrangements, room layout, position of the cake table and any tables required for displaying or serving food
- Establish the quantity and quality of the venue's furniture *(consider hiring tables and chairs, if necessary)*
- Determine whether an evening reception will necessitate a different room layout
- Check on food preparation area and refrigeration
- Discuss arrangements if you wish to display your wedding gifts
- Ask whether they can be kept in a safe place before and after the reception
- Advise your delivery and collection arrangements for the gifts
- Enquire about the provision of a marquee, if required – *see 'Marquees', page 137*
- Ask whether a public address system is available for the speeches
- Check on lighting, heating and ventilation
- Enquire whether a changing room is available
- Check on cloakroom and toilet facilities
- Check that there is adequate car parking space
- Check that there is easy access for any elderly or disabled guests
- Enquire about fire regulations and fire exits
- Check the venue has insurance cover for public liability

Decorations
- Discuss any plans you have to decorate the hall or room

Entertainment
- Establish whether entertainment is permitted
- If so, discuss your plans for a disco/live band/entertainment – *see 'Entertainment', page 157*
- Check on lighting, power supply and changing facilities
- Discuss background music playing during the meal, if required

Confirmation
- Discuss the estimated total cost and ascertain whether VAT has been included in the prices
- Request a detailed estimate in writing
- Confirm acceptance in writing and enclose the required deposit

One week before
- Telephone or call round to check final arrangements
- Confirm the final numbers and seating arrangements
- Prepare seating plan and write place name cards

Day before
- Decorate the hall or room
- Deliver wedding gifts, flowers, seating plan, place name cards and any necessary items

AT HOME

A reception at home will have a more intimate atmosphere, but numbers may be restricted. A marquee in the garden will offer more space and flexibility. Depending on the number of guests, you may wish to consider hiring professional caterers.

Refer to Checklist 26 'Reception – At Home', page 236

❑ Decide on the style of reception and number of guests
❑ Consider hiring a marquee – *see 'Marquees', page 137*
❑ Decide whether you will have additional guests in the evening
❑ Decide whether you will prepare the food yourself or hire professional caterers – *see 'Catering', page 138*

Number of Guests
* Reception
* Evening reception

Times
* Decide on the timings:
  * caterers arrive
  * arrival of guests
  * meal
  * speeches
  * cutting the cake
  * evening reception
  * entertainment
  * finish

Food and Drink

- Finger buffet • fork buffet • sit-down meal • barbecue
- Consider the provision of bar facilities

Facilities

- Decide on seating arrangements, room layout, position of the cake table and any tables required for displaying or serving food
- Consider whether you have sufficient tables and chairs *(consider hiring tables and chairs, if necessary)*
- Consider whether an evening reception will necessitate a different room layout
- Decide whether you wish to display your wedding gifts
- Arrange a table for the gifts
- Consider cloakroom and toilet facilities
- Consider the availability of adequate car parking space
- Check access for any elderly or disabled guests
- Identify any other risks such as poor lighting, uneven surfaces, etc.
- Check with your insurance company regarding public liability cover
- Establish whether any of your guests require overnight accommodation

Staff/Helpers

- Consider whether the caterers will provide all the necessary staff or you will arrange your own helpers

Flowers

- Determine whether the caterers will provide the flowers or you will supply your own
- Decide where you would like them placed

Decorations

- Decide what decorations you will have
- Consider whether you will need any help

Entertainment

- Decide whether you wish to have any entertainment – *see 'Entertainment', page 157*
- Consider lighting, power supply and changing facilities
- Decide whether you wish to have any background music

1 week

- Telephone caterers and suppliers to check final arrangements
- Confirm the final numbers
- Prepare seating plan and write place name cards, if appropriate

1 day

- Arrange the seating, and tables for displaying and serving the food
- Set up the wedding gift table
- Decorate the house
- Arrange flowers

MARQUEES

Hiring a marquee gives you the opportunity to welcome guests to a wedding reception at home if additional space is required. There are two types of marquee – traditional canvas tent with one or two supporting poles and guy ropes, and the aluminium frame tent, freestanding with no poles or ropes. The frame tent is more suitable for weddings, but the canvas one is slightly cheaper.

Refer to Checklist 27 'Marquees', page 238

❑ Identify hire companies *(see Yellow Pages or the Internet)*
❑ Request brochures and prices
❑ Arrange a site meeting to discuss your requirements:
   • size and style of marquee
   • style and colour of lining
   • flooring
     Coconut matting on the grass or boarded with either matting or carpet on top. Interlocking parquet is the best surface for dancing
   • tables and chairs
   • staging *(for wedding cake table, speeches, band or disco)*
   • heating and ventilation
   • lighting
   • exterior floodlighting
   • public address system for speeches
   • power supply
   • generator *(if additional electricity is needed)*
   • access to house

- covered walkways
- details of setting up and dismantling
- estimated total cost and payment details
- request a detailed estimate in writing
☐ Confirm acceptance in writing and pay the required deposit
☐ Decide on any special theme
☐ Decide on the provision of flowers – *see 'Flowers', page 66*
☐ Decide what decorations you will have

CATERING

Whether you choose professional caterers or prepare some of the food yourself, it is important to have the freedom to enjoy the reception and circulate among the guests. You need to consider a professional caterer if your guest list exceeds 20. You might not enjoy yourself if you're running around worrying about dirty dishes and whether or not everyone has had enough to eat.

Factors that determine your style of catering are:
- budget
- number of guests *(consider professional caterers if over 20)*
- availability of sufficient cutlery, china, glassware, etc.
- time of wedding *(tends to dictate how hungry your guests will be and the most appropriate type of food to provide)*
- type of food to be served
- help available for advance food preparation and on the day

OPTIONS

Self-catering
Prepare all the food and serve it yourself. It is advisable for your helpers at the reception not to be guests

Partial Self-catering
Prepare all the food, but hire serving staff on the day. Alternatively, have the food professionally prepared and serve it yourself

Professional Catering
All the food and serving staff are provided

SELF-CATERING
Good organisation is vital for successful self-catering. Once you have decided what food and drink you will serve, make a detailed action plan and allocate duties such as shopping, cooking, serving food and drinks, clearing away and washing-up.

Refer to Checklist 28 'Self-catering', page 240

❏ Decide how many helpers you will need to serve food and drinks
  1:15 helper-guest ratio for a buffet/1:10 helper-guest ratio for a served sit-down meal

Number of Guests

- Reception
- Evening reception
- Decide when final numbers are required

Times

- Food preparation
- Arrival of helpers
- Arrival of guests
- Meal
- Speeches
- Cutting the cake
- Evening reception
- Buffet
- Estimated finish
- Clearing away

Food

- Decide whether you will prepare all the food yourself or have any professionally prepared – *see 'Professional Catering', page 143*
- Provision of aperitifs and canapés on arrival
- Finger buffet • fork buffet • sit-down meal • barbecue
  Do not be over-ambitious. Avoid food that is very spicy, rich or fiddly to eat. Choose bite-size, non-drip and non-crumbly food for a finger buffet. It is advisable to test out any new recipes beforehand

- Decide what can be made in advance and will freeze well
- Special dietary requirements, e.g. kosher, vegetarian or allergies
  (produce signs for food that contain possible allergens)
- Decide on the menu and prepare a shopping list
- Arrange delivery of the wedding cake to reception venue, if appropriate

Drinks
- Drinks to be served on arrival
- Purchase wine, soft drinks, fruit juice and mineral water
  Many off-licences will supply wine on a sale-or-return basis
- Champagne or sparkling wine served with the cake
- Liqueurs, brandy, port served with the coffee
- Ice
- Decide who will serve the drinks

Helpers
- Shopping
- Cooking for the freezer
- Preparation of food, setting-up the bar, etc.
- Transportation of food and equipment to and from the venue
- Serving the food and drinks *(hire waiters/waitresses, if necessary)*
- Slicing the cake
- Handing out bridal favours
- Clearing away
- Washing-up

Equipment

- List requirements and decide what you will need to borrow or hire

  See your local Yellow Pages *or the internet for hire companies*
  - china • cutlery • glassware *(many off-licences will hire out glasses if you purchase the wine from them)*
  - tables and chairs
  - tablecloths and napkins
  - candelabra and candles
  - cake stand and knife
  - urn for boiling water
  - coffee/tea pots
  - heated trays
  - condiment sets
  - glass cloths
  - corkscrews and bottle openers
  - food thermometer and temperature probe for hot food
  - rubbish sacks
- Decide whether you will have sufficient fridge and freezer space. If not, approach people who may be able to offer some space

1 month

- Purchase ingredients and prepare food for the freezer
- Buy the wine, champagne, liqueurs, etc. and arrange to hire glassware

1 week
- Continue preparation of food
- Prepare or purchase ice cubes

1 day
- De-frost food
- Do last minute shopping for perishables
- Assemble all equipment and glassware
- Chill wine and drinks
- Arrange furniture and set up wedding gift table
- Lay table(s), apart from food

On the day
- Set out the food
- Open the wine
- Remind helpers to observe good catering practice, e.g. testing the temperature of hot food and removing unconsumed food to prevent possible contamination and food poisoning

PROFESSIONAL CATERING

The wedding meal is an important part of your wedding day and something you and your guests will remember. The key is to find a caterer who will create the perfect menu, at the right price and ensure the reception goes without a hitch.

Refer to Checklist 29 'Professional Catering', page 244

How to Choose a Caterer

❑ Identify suitable ones *(aim for at least three)*
  - personal experience   • recommendation   • good reputation   • advertisement   • *Yellow Pages*   • website
❑ Check their availability on the date you require
❑ Request brochures, sample menus and prices
❑ Ensure you are satisfied that they can meet all your requirements and cope with the number of guests
❑ Consider whether to ask for references and details of their qualifications
❑ Confirm their availability
❑ Arrange a meeting to discuss your requirements:
  - venue
  - style of reception
  - cost per head
  - ascertain whether they can offer a party-planning service and the cost
    Arrange marquee hire, flowers, toastmaster, entertainment, etc.

Number of Guests

- Reception
- Evening reception
- Ascertain when final numbers are required

Times

- Discuss the timings:
  - arrival at venue
  - arrival of guests
  - meal
  - speeches
  - cutting the cake
  - evening reception
  - buffet
  - bar closes
  - finish
  - clearing away

Facilities

- Discuss the room layout and seating arrangements
- Determine whether an evening reception will necessitate a change of room layout
- Discuss the provision of a seating plan and place name cards
- Discuss kitchen facilities, refrigeration, water and power supply
- Discuss delivery arrangements and parking
- Discuss cloakroom, toilet and changing facilities
- Confirm that they will remove the rubbish
- Establish they have public liability insurance cover

Equipment

- Discuss the provision of equipment:
  - china

- cutlery
- glassware
- cake-stand and knife
- tablecloths, napkins, candelabra, candles *(specify colour, if appropriate)*
- heated trays
- tables and chairs, including a table to display wedding gifts

Flowers

- Discuss whether they will provide the flowers or you will supply your own
- Specify type and colour of flowers, if appropriate
- Discuss where the flowers will be placed

Food

- Aperitifs and canapés to be served on arrival
- Finger buffet • fork buffet • sit-down meal • barbecue
- Evening reception
- Discuss menu and select from set menus or make your own suggestions
- Ascertain what quantity of food is included in the price
- Special dietary requirements, e.g. kosher, vegetarian or allergies
- Special menu/small portions for children
- Discuss delivery of the wedding cake, if appropriate
- Enquire what happens to any food left over *(re-plated or taken away)*

Drinks

- Served on arrival *(punch, kir, champagne, buck's fizz, sherry, fruit juice)*
- Wine(s) to be served with meal
- Soft drinks, fruit juice and mineral water
- Champagne or sparkling wine served with the cake
- Liqueurs, brandy, port served with the coffee
- Decide who will supply the wine and other drinks
- Enquire whether there is a corkage charge if you provide your own
  You could consider buying it on a sale-or-return basis from an off-licence
- Bar equipment and ice
- Specify the quantities to be served
- Enquire whether they have an alcohol licence if you plan to have a pay bar

Staff

- Agree how many staff will be provided for the number of guests
  - serving food • bar • cloakroom
  Staff-guest ratios: 1:15 for a buffet/1:10 for a served sit-down meal
- Enquire whether they will wear uniforms
- Provide any special instructions, e.g. cutting and distribution of the cake

- Request bridal favours, e.g. sugared almonds, be handed out to guests
- Enquire whether they can provide a Master of Ceremonies/ Toastmaster, if required

Cost

- Establish whether service charge is included or if gratuities are optional
- Check whether a charge is made for cleaning the room or hall after the function
- Enquire whether VAT is included in the prices
- Determine whether there is a charge if the reception overruns
- Ascertain whether there is a surcharge for small numbers
- Determine their terms for breakages

Confirmation

- Request a detailed breakdown of charges
  Food, drinks, corkage, staff, service charge, delivery, travelling expenses, equipment hire, party planning, etc.
- Confirm acceptance of estimate in writing and pay the required deposit

1 week

- Telephone or arrange a meeting to check final arrangements
- Confirm final numbers
- Provide seating plan and place name cards
- Arrange access to venue
- Exchange mobile telephone numbers for use on the day

WEDDING CAKE

The wedding cake is the centrepiece of your reception and cutting the cake is one of the traditional highlights. Your first decision is what type of wedding cake to have and whether you will make it yourself or have it professionally made.

Refer to Checklist 30 'Wedding Cake', page 247

☐ Decide on your requirements
  - one cake or individual ones
  - type of cake *(fruit, sponge or chocolate)*
  - number of slices required *(taking into account the number of guests, number of portions to be sent out in cake boxes and whether you wish to keep a tier for Christmas or the first christening)* or how many individual cakes
  - configuration
    - two-tiered cake 8″ and 10″ or 10″ and 12″
    - three-tiered cake 6″, 8″ and 10″ or 8″, 10″ and 12″
  - shape
  - colour and type of icing
  - additional decoration
  - cake-stand and knife *(this may be provided by the caterers, hotel or restaurant, or can be hired from a professional bakers)*

Size of cake		No. of slices (fruit cake)	No. of slices (sponge cake)
13cm/5″	round	14	7
	square	16	8
15cm/6″	round	22	11
	square	27	14
18cm/7″	round	30	15
	square	40	20
20cm/8″	round	40	20
	square	54	27
23cm/9″	round	54	27
	square	70	35
25cm/10″	round	68	34
	square	90	45
27cm/11″	round	86	43
	square	112	56
30cm/12″	round	100	50
	square	134	67

These figures are intended as a rough guide only and should be checked with your baker

Professionally-made Cake
❑ Choose a baker
- recommendation • good reputation • advertisement
- website
- ask if samples of cake are available

❑ Discuss your requirements in detail
   Most professional bakers have a selection of colour
   photographs of cake designs
❑ Decide whether you wish to collect the cake or have it
   delivered
❑ Ascertain the total cost, amount of deposit and delivery
   charge
❑ Arrange to hire a cake-stand and knife, if required
❑ Arrange to see the finished cake a week before the wedding
❑ Arrange for delivery to the reception venue

Home-made Cake
❑ List and purchase ingredients
❑ Bake cakes
   Traditional wedding cake should be made at least three
   months before icing and decoration
❑ Marzipan or almond paste *(two weeks before icing)*
❑ Icing
❑ Additional decoration
   Piped flowers, bells, figures, etc. can be obtained from some
   specialist bakers or kitchen utensil shops
❑ Arrange to hire a cake-stand and knife, if required
❑ Arrange for delivery to the reception venue

SPEECHES

Unless someone is an accomplished after dinner speaker or is very familiar with addressing groups of people, they may regard giving a speech an ordeal. However, with careful planning and by following a few simple guidelines any fears should soon be allayed.

There are three main purposes of wedding speeches – to congratulate the couple by wishing them every happiness in their life together, to thank the appropriate people and to propose toasts.

The speeches are given after the meal and usually before the cutting of the cake. Following each toast, all guests should stand, raise their glasses, repeat the toast and drink to whoever was mentioned.

SPEECHES AND TOASTS

Usually three speeches are given – by the giver-away of the bride, the bridegroom and the best man – and these include the toasts. Although there is no need for the bride to make a speech, she may wish to say a few words. In which case, she would probably speak after the groom. The speeches are traditionally announced by the toastmaster, Master of Ceremonies or the best man.

First speech

The first speech is given by the giver-away (usually the bride's father). It is about the bride and is best kept brief and fairly serious.

Traditionally, it contains words of affection and praise for his daughter and perhaps one or two stories about her childhood and adolescence. In welcoming his new son-in-law into the family, he expresses his (and his wife's) happiness in getting to know him and his family. He declares his confidence in the couple's future happiness and wishes them a long and successful marriage. In conclusion he proposes a toast to the bride and groom.

Second speech

The groom responds on behalf of the bride and himself. The tone of this speech is straightforward and sincere. He begins by thanking the bride's father for proposing the toast.

He pays tribute to his wife's parents for the way in which they have brought up their daughter and expresses his happiness at having such a lovely wife. At this point he may also wish to thank his parents for their love and support.

He may talk about how they met and his intentions to ensure their future happiness together. He should thank the bride's parents, or whoever is hosting the occasion, for a wonderful day and for their generosity.

It is important to say what a pleasure it is to see so many family and friends gathered together, and to thank them for their good wishes and generous gifts. He closes by thanking his best man, the bridesmaids, the pageboys and anyone else who has contributed towards the success of the day and proposes a toast to the bridesmaids and pageboys.

Third speech

The best man gives the final speech. If he is a confident speaker, he can make his speech witty and amusing. However, he must be careful it does not become embarrassing or in bad taste.

He begins by thanking the groom for the toast to the bridesmaids and then offers his congratulations to the bride and groom, wishing them every happiness for the future. At this stage he may tell an amusing story or two about the groom's schooldays or adolescent years, particularly if there is any shared history between them. He could also relate how the couple first met. He may propose a toast to any absent friends and then read out any greetings cards, emails and telemessages. Finally, he announces the cutting of the cake.

PREPARATION

There is no substitute for careful planning and preparation. Decide on the length of the speech and then break it up into small sections, by noting all the points to be covered and allocating the time accordingly. By prioritising and ordering the points logically, a framework will easily be developed. Consider the use of props to add variety and humour.

The best method to practise and deliver a speech is by writing the key points on cue cards. A separate word should be written boldly and highlighted on a plain card, perhaps with a few memory-joggers. Each of the cards should be numbered.

PRESENTATION

To ensure success three main areas should be considered – words, voice and body language.

Choose the right words to convey the message and consider including some quotations that can be used as an introduction, perhaps to an amusing story.

The voice can be used to add meaning and emphasis. Speaking in a leisurely manner and varying tone and volume will avoid it sounding monotonous. Pauses can be a powerful way of getting attention and adding emphasis, as well as giving time to take a breath and collect one's thoughts. If you are nervous, try and think of your breathing so you do not mumble and so that everyone in the room can hear you. Speak in a natural accent and not too quickly.

Keep your gestures natural and restrained, avoiding the tendency to fiddle with props or cue cards. Use eye contact and stand with feet slightly apart, turning your body from time to time to face all the audience.

SUMMARY

- Plan the content and prepare cue cards.
- Time your speech and be brief – five minutes is ample.
- Rehearse in front of a mirror, video or a close but critical friend.
- Do not swear, blaspheme or tell lies.
- Do not tell embarrassing stories, repeat crude jokes or say anything of a sensitive nature that may cause offence.
- Enjoy giving your speech, keep to time and to your planned script. Speaking in front of a live audience will transform a carefully prepared speech into a great one and everyone will appreciate your efforts.

ENTERTAINMENT

Entertainment is a huge part of your wedding reception to ensure everyone enjoys the celebrations in a great party atmosphere. Whether you want a DJ, a live band or pre-recorded music, there's great scope for letting your imagination run wild.

Refer to Checklist 31 'Entertainment', page 249

❑ Decide whether you wish to have any entertainment at the reception
  - disco
  - live band
  - musicians
  - pre-recorded music
  - entertainers *(particularly for any children, e.g. a clown, magician, puppet theatre or a video)*

❑ Obtain permission of the venue manager

❑ Check that the venue holds an entertainments licence

❑ Check on lighting, power supply and any changing facilities

❑ Identify suitable discos/bands/entertainers/musicians
  - personal experience   • recommendation   • advertisement
  - website

❑ Check on their availability on the date you require

❑ Obtain brochures and prices

❑ Arrange a meeting to discuss your requirements:
  - details and time of setting-up and dismantling

- start and finish times
- number and times of breaks
- music for the first dance
- special requests
- special instructions *(type of music, volume, tempo, etc.)*
- cancellation fee
- estimated total cost and whether VAT is payable
❏ Request an estimate in writing
❏ Confirm acceptance in writing and enclose the required deposit
❏ Telephone to check final arrangements one week before reception
❏ Exchange mobile telephone numbers for use on the day

ACCOMMODATION AND HOSPITALITY

If you have guests travelling from a distance who need to stay overnight, any local knowledge and help you can offer to simplify the arrangements will be much appreciated.

On the wedding day itself, you may want to offer light refreshments at home depending on the time of the ceremony.

ACCOMMODATION

❑ Arrange overnight accommodation for family and guests, if required
  • at a hotel *(you may be able to negotiate a group discount)*
  • with nearby friends or neighbours
❑ Confirm all arrangements in writing
  • date   • time of arrival   • length of stay   • cost
❑ Send a copy of the confirmation to relevant guests
❑ Produce a schedule with the suggested columns

| | | | | | | Date Confirmed |
Name of Guest	Name of Hotel or Neighbour	Length of Stay	Date(s)	Cost	Hotel/ Neighbour	Guest

❑ Alternatively, provide guests with a list of nearby hotels and guesthouses with prices

❑ Buy small token of appreciation if neighbours provide accommodation

HOSPITALITY

❑ Arrange light refreshments at home on the wedding day for bridal party, attendants, photographer, etc.

❑ Decide whether any additional hospitality will be offered other than on the wedding day

❑ Make any appropriate arrangements

❑ Produce a schedule with the suggested columns

Date	Time	Name	Food	Drink

STAG AND HEN PARTIES

Although it's really the best man's job to make all the stag night arrangements and the hen night is the responsibility of the chief bridesmaid, if you have strong ideas on what you want to do – or definitely don't want to do – let them know firmly and early on. So choose well! Make sure you've discussed what kind of event you want to have beforehand.

Refer to Checklist 32 'Stag and Hen Parties', page 251

❏ Decide on the type of party and the venue
❏ Book the venue
❏ Arrange any catering
❏ Book any entertainment
❏ Compile an invitation list with the suggested columns

Name	Address/Telephone	Invited ✓	Reply ✓ or ✗

❏ Send out invitations and record responses as they arrive
❏ Arrange transport, if required

HONEYMOON

After all the planning, tension and hard work, it's time for you both to get away from it all and relax. It's the perfect way to reward yourselves and the first chance you'll get to spend some time together as man and wife away from your families and friends, so it's important to get it right.

Refer to Checklist 33 'Honeymoon', page 253

❑ Decide whether guests will contribute to the cost of your honeymoon or you will pay for it yourself

❑ Set a provisional budget
- 'holiday of a lifetime!' or less extravagant
- length of stay

❑ Discuss the type of holiday you both will enjoy
- on the beach • sightseeing • touring • other

❑ Identify suitable destinations
- UK • abroad

❑ Select the type of accommodation
- hotel • self-catering apartment • villa • other

❑ Decide on preferred method of travel
- air • sea • rail • road

❑ Decide how you wish to book your honeymoon
- holiday company • travel agent • website
  As a honeymoon couple, you may be entitled to a special discount/upgrade/champagne/flowers

❏ Arrange overnight accommodation on the wedding night, if required

❏ Decide whether to change the name in your passport
Some countries will not accept a passport that has not been amended (i.e. it is still in your maiden name), even if you carry your marriage certificate with you. Therefore, you must arrange to have a post-dated passport issued in your married name

❏ Obtain the necessary form signed by the officiant or Superintendent Registrar

❏ Send to the appropriate Passport Office. *Your new passport will only be valid from the date of your wedding since it will be post-dated. It is possible to apply up to three months in advance, but allow a minimum of six weeks for it to be processed*

❏ Arrange any necessary visas and check they can be stamped in a post-dated passport. *If a visa cannot be stamped in your post-dated passport, you will need to travel using a passport in your maiden name. As a precaution, take your marriage certificate with you if the tickets are booked in your married name*

❏ Purchase maps, guidebooks and any GPS upgrades

❏ Book the honeymoon in the name that will match your passport

❏ Arrange for full travel/medical insurance and apply for a European Health Insurance Card *(European destinations only)*

❏ Order currency and travellers' cheques

❑ Consult your GP regarding any advised or necessary inoculations or medicines at least three weeks prior to your proposed departure date

❑ Ensure you have an adequate supply of regularly taken medication and precautionary items

❑ Check on the amount and weight of luggage that you are allowed to take

❑ Prepare an emergency kit in your hand luggage in the event that your luggage is mislaid or delayed reaching your destination

❑   • washbag   • change of underwear and clothes
     • medication

❑ Make arrangements for any pets

❑ Arrange transport to and from the honeymoon departure point

❑ Advise neighbours of your itinerary and arrange for someone to check on your property while you are away

❑ Cancel newspaper delivery

❑ Cancel milk delivery

❑ Water houseplants

AFTER THE WEDDING

Now that the formalities have been concluded, all that remains are some administrative tasks such as informing relevant people and organisations of your change of name, thanking all the people who helped make the day run smoothly and ordering the wedding photographs.

Refer to Checklist 34 'After the Wedding', page 256

❑ Obtain some photocopies of your marriage certificate, as many organisations will require a copy when you notify them of your change of name

❑ Advise any change of name and address
There is no legal requirement for the bride to change her name. She can retain her own name completely, or continue to use it for business purposes only

❑ Write outstanding thank-you letters for wedding gifts or donations and note the date on which you send them

Gift or Donation	Given By/Promised By	Thank-you Sent (date)

❑ Write thank-you letters
  • parents • attendants • officiant • suppliers • helpers

❑ Arrange for bouquet to be dried, pressed or mounted, if required

❏ Send out a piece of cake, an order of service sheet or a DVD of the ceremony to people who could not attend the wedding

❏ Produce a schedule with the suggested columns

Name and Address	Cake	Order of Service	Date Sent

❏ Return any damaged or unwanted wedding gifts

❏ Produce a schedule with the suggested columns

Gift	Given By	Purchased From	Date Returned

❏ Obtain photograph proofs or view online

❏ Produce a schedule with the suggested columns

Name and Address	Tel. No.	Proof No.	Size	Qty.	Cost

❏ Select photographs and place order

❏ Collect and pay for video or DVD

❏ Pay outstanding invoices – *see Checklist 2 'Wedding Expenses', pages 172–183*

❏ Arrange press report and photograph

❏ Entertain both sets of parents, attendants and helpers

❏ Make a will or revise existing one
Marriage automatically invalidates a will made earlier

CHECKLISTS

Checklist 1   Wedding Fact File

Date_____ Time_____

Church/Register Office/Approved Premises

Officiant/Registrar/CPO_____

Address_____

Telephone_____ Fax_____

Email_____ Website_____

Best Man

Name_____ Mobile_____

Address_____ Email_____

_____ Telephone_____

Chief Bridesmaid/Matron of Honour

Name_____ Mobile_____

Address_____ Email_____

_____ Telephone_____

Bridesmaid(s)

1 Name_____ Mobile_____

   Address _____ Email_____

   _____ Telephone_____

2 Name_____ Mobile_____

   Address_____ Email_____

   _____ Telephone_____

3 Name_____ Mobile_____

   Address_____ Email_____

   _____ Telephone_____

Checklist 1   Wedding Fact File (Cont.)

Flower Girl

Name_____   Mobile_____

Address_____   Email_____

_____   Telephone_____

Pageboys

1 Name_____   Mobile_____

   Address_____   Email_____

   _____   Telephone_____

2 Name_____   Mobile_____

   Address_____   Email_____

   _____   Telephone_____

Ushers

1 Name_____   Mobile_____

   Address_____   Email_____

   _____   Telephone_____

2 Name_____   Mobile_____

   Address_____   Email_____

   _____   Telephone_____

3 Name_____   Mobile_____

   Address_____   Email_____

   _____   Telephone_____

4 Name_____   Mobile_____

   Address_____   Email_____

   _____   Telephone_____

Checklist 1   Wedding Fact File (Cont.)

Witnesses

1 Name_____ Mobile_____

   Address_____ Email_____

   _____ Telephone_____

2 Name_____ Mobile_____

   Address_____ Email_____

   _____ Telephone_____

Reception

Venue_____

Address_____

_____

Telephone_____ Fax_____

Email_____ Website_____

Contact_____

Honeymoon

Destination_____

Date_____ To_____

Telephone_____ Fax_____

Email_____ Website_____

Checklist 2	Wedding Expenses
Wedding Rings	Bride
	Groom
	Engraving
Church Ceremony	Officiant's fees
	Banns
	Marriage certificate
	Organist/choir
	Musicians
	Singers
	Bell-ringers
	Other
Civil Ceremony	Notices of intention
	Registrar's/CPO's fees
	Ceremony on approved premises
	Certificate of Marriage
Flowers	Ceremony
	Bride
	Bouquet
	Headdress
	Bridesmaids
	Bouquets
	Headdresses

Budget £	Estimate/Quotation £	Actual £	Deposit £	Balance £	Paid (date)

Checklist 2	Wedding Expenses (Cont.)
	Flower Girl
	Basket
	Headdress
	Corsages
	Buttonholes
	Reception
	Other
Photography/Video	Photographer's fees
	Prints or CDs of photographs
	Wedding album(s)
	Videographer's fees
	DVD copies
Transport	To ceremony
	To reception
	Going-away
	Gratuities
	Other
Stationery	Invitations
	Postage
	Order of service sheets
	Bridal favours
	Cake boxes
	Guest book
	Invitation reply cards

Budget £	Estimate/Quotation £	Actual £	Deposit £	Balance £	Paid (date)

Checklist 2	Wedding Expenses (Cont.)
	Keepsake album
	Menus/place name cards
	Personalised items
	Thank-you cards or letters
	Postage
	Other
Gifts	Bride
	Groom
	Chief Bridesmaid/Matron of Honour
	Bridesmaids
	Flower Girl
	Pageboys
	Best man
	Ushers
	Helpers
Clothes	Bride
	Wedding dress/outfit
	Veil/headdress/hat
	Shoes
	Accessories
	Lingerie
	Going-away outfit
	Matron of Honour
	Dress

Budget £	Estimate/Quotation £	Actual £	Deposit £	Balance £	Paid (date)

Checklist 2   Wedding Expenses (Cont.)

	Accessories
	Bridesmaids and Flower Girl
	Dresses
	Accessories
	Pageboys
	Outfits
	Accessories
	Male Attendants
	Hire of suits/morning dress
	Accessories
	Bridegroom
	Hire of suit/morning dress
	Accessories
	Going-away outfit
Clothes for the Honeymoon	Bride
	Groom
Hair and Beauty	Health spa or beauty salon
	Hairdressing for bride
	Beauty treatments/make-up artist
	Cosmetics/perfume
	Hairdressing for groom
Reception	Hire of hall or room
	Marquee
	Hire of furniture/equipment

Budget £	Estimate/Quotation £	Actual £	Deposit £	Balance £	Paid (date)

Checklist 2	Wedding Expenses (Cont.)
	Food
	Drinks/bar
	Wedding cake
	Staff and gratuities
	Entertainment
	Decorations
	Overnight accommodation
	Other
Honeymoon	Travel
	Hotel or other accommodation
	Travel insurance
	Taxis
	Spending money
	Passports/visas/maps
	Inoculations
	Other
Miscellaneous	Wedding insurance
	Accommodation for guests
	Hospitality and refreshments
	Press announcements
	Before/after the wedding
	Stag party
	Hen party
	Petty cash for best man

Budget £	Estimate/Quotation £	Actual £	Deposit £	Balance £	Paid (date)

Checklist 2   Wedding Expenses (Cont.)

Summary of Wedding Expenses

Wedding Rings

Church Ceremony

Civil Ceremony

Flowers

Photography/Video

Transport

Stationery

Gifts

Clothes

Clothes for the Honeymoon

Hair and Beauty

Reception

Honeymoon

Miscellaneous

TOTAL

Budget £	Estimate/Quotation £	Actual £	Deposit £	Balance £	Paid (date)

Checklist 3　　Wedding Rings

Supplier_____

Address_____

_____

_____

Telephone_____

Email_____ Website_____

Contact_____

Bride's Ring

Date ordered_____

Details to be engraved_____

_____

_____

Jeweller's valuation £_____

Insurance cover arranged_____

Date for collection_____

Deposit £_____ Date paid_____

Balance £_____ Date paid_____

Groom's Ring

Date ordered_____

Details to be engraved_____

_____

_____

Checklist 3   Wedding Rings (Cont.)

Jeweller's valuation £_____

Insurance cover arranged_____

Date for collection_____

Deposit £_____   Date paid_____

Balance £_____   Date paid_____

Checklist 4   Church Wedding

Church_____

Officiant_____

Address_____

_____

Telephone_____ Fax_____

Email_____ Website_____

Date of wedding_____ Time_____

Musician(s)_____

Singer(s)_____

Organist_____

Telephone_____

Other weddings on the same day_____

Flowers_____

_____

_____

Policy on photographs/video_____

_____

_____

Policy on confetti_____

Dates for preparation classes or instruction_____

Dates for Banns to be read in bride's church_____

1_____ 2_____ 3_____

Dates for Banns to be read in groom's church if appropriate

1_____ 2_____ 3_____

Date of rehearsal_____ Time_____

Checklist 4   Church Wedding (Cont.)

Church Fees

Officiant_____ £_____

Banns_____ £_____

Marriage Certificate_____ £_____

Organist_____ £_____

Choir_____ £_____

Bell-ringers_____ £_____

Video recording copyright_____ £_____

Total_____ **£**_____

Details of payment_____

Musician(s)/singer(s)_____ £_____

Flowers_____ £_____

Checklist 5   Order of Service

Medley of music before the bride arrives_____

_____

_____

_____

_____

Processional_____

_____

Officiant's introduction_____

*Hymn/Psalm*_____

*Bible Reading(s)*_____

_____

Marriage ceremony, including vows_____

*Bible Reading(s)*_____

_____

Address_____

*Hymn/Psalm*_____

Prayers and responses_____

_____

_____

*Holy Communion*_____

Blessing_____

Music during the signing of the register_____

_____

_____

_____

_____

Checklist 5   Order of Service (Cont.)

Performances by   * choir   * musician(s)   * singer(s)_____

_____

_____

_____

Recessional_____

_____

Items in italics are optional

Checklist 6   Civil Ceremony – Register Office

Register Office_____

Address_____

_____

Telephone_____ Fax_____

Email_____ Website_____

Superintendent Registrar_____

Registrar/CPO_____

Date of ceremony_____ Time_____

Number of guests_____

Extra declarations or poetry readings_____

_____

Music of your choice_____

Policy on confetti_____

Policy on photographs/video/webcam_____

_____

Flowers_____

Car parking_____

Witnesses

1_____

2_____

Checklist 6   Civil Ceremony – Register Office (Cont.)

Fees

Notices of intention_____ £_____

Superintendent Registrar's/Registrar's/CPO's fees_____ £_____

Certificate of Marriage_____ £_____

Total_____ **£**_____

Service of Blessing   ☐ Yes   ☐ No

Checklist 7   Civil Ceremony – Approved Premises

Venue_____

Address_____

_____

_____

Telephone_____ Fax_____

Email_____ Website_____

Contact_____

Date of ceremony_____ Time_____

Room for ceremony_____

Room(s) for reception_____

Number of guests_____

Other ceremonies on the same day_____

Flowers_____

_____

_____

_____

Policy on confetti_____

Car parking_____

_____

Hire of room(s)_____ £_____

Exclusive use_____ £_____

Flowers_____ £_____

Total_____ **£**_____

Deposit £_____ Date paid_____

Balance £_____ Date paid_____

Checklist 7   Civil Ceremony – Approved Premises (Cont.)

Date of confirmation (sent/received)_____

Superintendent Registrar_____

Registrar/CPO_____

Extra declarations or poetry readings_____

_____

_____

_____

_____

Music of your choice_____

_____

_____

_____

_____

Policy on photographs/video_____

_____

_____

_____

_____

Witnesses

1_____

2_____

Checklist 7   Civil Ceremony – Approved Premises (Cont.)

Fees

Notices of intention_____ £_____

Superintendent Registrar's/Registrar's/CPO's fees_____ £_____

Certificate of Marriage_____ £_____

Total_____ **£**_____

Service of Blessing   ☐ Yes   ☐ No

Checklist 8   Marrying Abroad

Travel agent/holiday company_____

Address_____

_____

Telephone_____ Fax_____

Email_____ Website_____

Wedding location_____

Address_____

_____

Contact_____ Telephone_____

Email_____ Website_____

Date of ceremony_____ Time_____

Period of residency_____

Requirements for Wedding

Wedding insurance_____

Transportation costs to the resort authorities_____

Marriage Licence and Certificate_____

Services of the Registrar_____

Wedding cake and hors d'oeuvres_____

Sparkling wine or champagne_____

Bouquet and buttonhole_____

Additional flowers and decorations_____

Musicians_____

Photographs_____

Video_____

Checklist 8   Marrying Abroad (Cont.)

Documentation Required

❑ Passports
❑ Birth certificates
❑ Decree Absolute if divorced
❑ Death certificate if widowed
❑ Proof of change of name by Deed Poll
❑ Parental consent (depending on your age)
❑ Adoption certificate
❑ Passport photographs
❑ Photocopies of documents prior to travel
❑ All original documents to be taken out to resort
❑ Translations of foreign documents to be taken out to resort
Additional requirements_____

Checklist 9   Service of Blessing

Church_____

Officiant_____

Address_____

_____

Telephone_____ Fax_____

Email_____ Website_____

Date of ceremony_____ Time_____

Musician(s)_____

Singer(s)_____

Organist_____

Telephone_____

Other services on the same day_____

_____

_____

Flowers_____

_____

_____

Policy on photographs/video_____

_____

Date of rehearsal_____ Time_____

Church Fees

Officiant_____ £_____

Organist_____ £_____

Choir_____ £_____

Bell-ringers_____ £_____

Checklist 9   Service of Blessing (Cont.)

Video recording copyright_____ £_____

Total_____ **£**_____

Details of payment_____

Musician(s)_____ £_____

Singer(s)_____ £_____

Flowers_____ £_____

Checklist 10   Flowers

Florist_____

Address_____

_____

Telephone_____   Mobile_____

Email_____   Website_____

Contact_____

Colour scheme_____

General style_____

Favourite flowers_____

Bride's Bouquet

Colour_____

Style_____

Bride's Headdress *(also discuss with hairdresser)*

Colour_____

Style_____

Chief Bridesmaid/Matron of Honour's Bouquet

Colour_____

Style_____

Chief Bridesmaid/Matron of Honour's Headdress

(also discuss with hairdresser)

Colour_____

Style_____

Bridesmaids' Bouquets

Colour_____

Checklist 10   Flowers (Cont.)

Style_____

Number_____

Bridesmaids' Headdresses *(also discuss with hairdresser)*

Colour_____

Style_____

Number_____

Basket of Flowers for the Flower Girl

Colour_____

Style_____

Mothers' Corsages *(check colour of clothes)*

Bride's mother

Colour_____

Style_____

Groom's mother

Colour_____

Style_____

Buttonholes

Groom/best man/fathers_____ Colour_____ No._____

Pageboys_____ Colour_____ No._____

Ushers_____ Colour_____ No._____

Guests_____ Colour_____ No._____

Delivery date_____ Time_____

Delivery address_____

Checklist 10   Flowers (Cont.)

Church *(also discuss with the officiant whether any flowers are provided and if there are any other weddings on the same day)*

Colour_____

Style_____

Church entrance_____

Altar_____

Chancel steps_____

Pulpit_____

Lectern_____

Pew ends_____

Windowsills_____

Columns_____

Font_____

Delivery date_____   Time_____

Delivery address_____

_____   _____

_____

Civil Ceremony

Colour_____

Style_____

Delivery date_____   Time_____

Delivery address_____

_____

_____

Checklist 10   Flowers (Cont.)

Reception *(also discuss with hotel/restaurant/hall/caterers)*

Colour_____

Style_____

Entrance_____

Buffet table_____

Dining tables_____

Cake table_____

Delivery date_____ Time_____

Delivery address_____

_____

_____

Estimated Cost

Bouquets_____ £_____

Basket_____ £_____

Headdresses_____ £_____

Corsages_____ £_____

Buttonholes_____ £_____

Church/civil ceremony_____ £_____

Reception_____ £_____

Total_____ **£**_____

Deposit £_____ Date paid_____

Date for balance to be paid_____ Date paid_____

Address for invoice_____

_____

_____

Checklist 11   Photography

Name of photographer/studio_____

Address_____

_____ Mobile_____

Telephone_____ Fax_____

Email_____ Website_____

Attendance fee_____

Package details_____

Cost of photographs £_____ CD £_____

Online images available by_____

Proofs ready by_____

Album ready by_____

Details of online images URL/password_____

Pictures at Home
Time of arrival_____

At the Church/Register Office/Approved Premises
Time of arrival_____

Location_____

At the Reception
Time of arrival_____

Location_____

Checklist 11   Photography (Cont.)

Additional photographs *(e.g. during speeches, guests, head table, guests at tables, informal pictures of guests mingling, dancing, bride throwing bouquet, leaving for honeymoon)*

_____

_____

_____

Any special effects required_____

_____

Deposit £_____ Date paid_____

Balance £_____ Date paid_____

Checklist 12   Video

Videographer_____

Address_____

_____ Mobile_____

Telephone_____ Fax_____

Email_____ Website_____

Additional sound-track_____

Edited highlights_____

Number of copies required   DVD_____ Cost £_____

Delivery date_____

Pictures at Home

Time of arrival_____

Final preparations

Being photographed

Leaving house

At the Church/Register Office/Approved Premises

Time of arrival_____ Location_____

Arriving at church/register office/approved premises

Bride walking up the aisle with father

During the Ceremony *(if permitted)*

Hymns *(church only)*

Vows

Singers/musicians *(church only)*

Signing the register/schedule

Coming down the aisle

Checklist 12   Video (Cont.)

Outside the Church/Register Office/Approved Premises
Greeting guests
During photographs
Throwing of confetti
Leaving for reception

At the Reception
Time of arrival_____ Location_____
Greeting guests
Speeches
Cutting the cake
First dance
Going away
Deposit £_____ Date paid_____
Balance £_____ Date paid_____

Checklist 13   Transport

Hire company_____

Address_____

_____ Mobile_____

Telephone_____ Fax_____

Email_____ Website_____

Name of contact_____

Number of vehicles_____

Type/colour_____

Flowers/decoration_____

To collect bridesmaids, pageboys, bride's mother

Time_____

To collect bride and bride's father

Time_____

To take bride, groom and attendants to reception

Time_____

Ceremony venue_____

_____

Reception venue_____

_____

Extras *(champagne, etc.)*

Total cost £_____

Deposit £_____ Date paid_____

Balance £_____ Date paid_____

Checklist 13   Transport (Cont.)

Details of any Borrowed Cars

Name_____   Name_____

Address_____   Address_____

_____   _____

Telephone_____   Telephone_____

Details of Lifts arranged to the Ceremony/Reception_____

_____

_____

Transport for Going-away_____

_____

_____

Checklist 14   Stationery

Name of supplier/printer_____
Address_____
_____

Telephone_____ Fax_____
Email_____ Website_____

	No.	**Cost**
Invitations_____	_____	£_____

*One per couple or family (children over
18 should receive their own invitation),
officiant, parents, best man, ushers,
attendants and a few spares*

| **Evening invitations**_____ | _____ | £_____ |
| **Order of service sheets**_____ | _____ | £_____ |

Officiant _____ *organist*_____ *members of choir*_____
guests _____ *mementoes*_____

Miscellaneous

Book matches_____	_____	£_____
Bottle neck labels_____	_____	£_____
Bridal favours_____	_____	£_____
Cake boxes_____	_____	£_____
Crackers_____	_____	£_____
Drink mats_____	_____	£_____
Guest book_____	_____	£_____
Invitation reply cards_____	_____	£_____
Keepsake album_____	_____	£_____

Checklist 14   Stationery (Cont.)

Menu cards_____   _____   £_____

Paper plates_____   _____   £_____

Personalised celebration balloons_____   _____   £_____

Personalised Holy Bibles (yourselves,
parents, helpers)_____   _____   £_____

Personalised satin ribbons (tables, pews,
wedding cars)_____   _____   £_____

Personalised video/DVD cases_____   _____   £_____

Photograph album(s) or digital image CDs   _____   £_____

Photograph wallets (for informal
snapshots)_____   _____   £_____

Place name cards_____   _____   £_____

Serviettes/serviette rings_____   _____   £_____

Thank you cards or letters_____   _____   £_____

Checklist 15   Wedding Gifts

Wedding Gift List and Bridal Account Card

Store_____

Address_____

Telephone_____ Fax_____

Email_____ Website_____

Contact_____

Account details_____

Total amount received £_____

Store_____

Address_____

Telephone_____ Fax_____

Email_____ Website_____

Contact_____

Account details_____

Total amount received £_____

Honeymoon Fund

Holiday company_____

Address_____

Telephone_____ Fax_____

Email_____ Website_____

Contact_____

Account details_____

Total amount received £_____

Checklist 15   Wedding Gifts (Cont.)

Charity Donations

Name of Charity_____

Website_____

Total amount received £_____

Name of Charity_____

Website_____

Total amount received £_____

Checklist 16   Clothes for the Bride

Supplier/dressmaker_____

Address_____

_____

Telephone_____   Fax_____

Email_____   Website_____

Dress/Outfit

Colour_____

Style_____

_____

Bodice/neckline_____

Waist/sash_____

Sleeves_____

Shape of skirt_____

Length/hemline_____

Embroidery/trimmings_____

Fabric_____

Lining_____

Pattern No._____

Size/measurements_____

Dates for fittings_____

Dates for alterations_____

Date for collection_____

Checklist 16   Clothes for the Bride (Cont.)

Cost £_____ Payment details_____

Deposit £_____ Date paid_____

Balance £_____ Date paid_____

Hire Details

Items to be hired_____

Cost £_____

Dates for fittings_____

Date for collection_____

To be returned by_____ Date for return_____

Deposit £_____ Date paid_____

Balance £_____ Date paid_____

Headdress

Colour_____

Style_____

Fabric_____

Embroidery/trimmings_____

Veil_____

Cost £_____ Payment details_____

Accessories

Shoes_____ Cost £_____

Underwear_____ Cost £_____

Hosiery_____ Cost £_____

Gloves_____ Cost £_____

Jewellery_____ Cost £_____

Checklist 16   Clothes for the Bride (Cont.)

Other_____ Cost £_____

Total_____ Cost £_____

Something Old_____

New_____

Borrowed_____

Blue_____

Going-away Outfit

_____

_____

_____

Accessories

_____

_____

_____

Cost £_____ Payment details____ _____

Checklist 17   Clothes for the Matron of Honour

Supplier/dressmaker_____

Address_____

_____

Telephone_____ Fax_____

Email_____ Website_____

Outfit

Colour_____

Style_____

Bodice/neckline_____

Waist_____

Sleeves_____

Shape of skirt_____

Length/hemline_____

Embroidery/trimmings_____

Fabric_____

Lining_____

Pattern No._____

Size/measurements_____

Dates for fittings_____

Dates for alterations_____

Date for collection_____

Cost £_____ Payment details_____

Deposit £_____ Date paid_____

Balance £_____ Date paid_____

Checklist 17   Clothes for the Matron of Honour (Cont.)

Hire Details

Items to be hired_____ Cost £_____

Dates for fittings_____

Date for collection_____

To be returned by_____ Date for return_____

Deposit £_____ Date paid_____

Balance £_____ Date paid_____

Headdress

Style/flowers_____

Cost £_____ Payment details_____

Accessories

Shoes_____ Cost £_____

Hosiery_____ Cost £_____

Jewellery_____ Cost £_____

Checklist 18   Clothes for the Bridesmaids

Supplier/dressmaker_____

Address_____

_____

Telephone_____ Fax_____

Email_____ Website_____

Dress

Colour_____

Style_____

Bodice/neckline_____

Waist/sash_____

Sleeves_____

Shape of skirt_____

Length/hemline_____

Embroidery/trimmings_____

Fabric_____

Lining_____

Pattern No._____

Size/measurements_____

Dates for fittings_____

Dates for alterations_____

Date for collection_____

Cost £_____ Payment details_____

Deposit £_____ Date paid_____

Balance £_____ Date paid_____

Checklist 18   Clothes for the Bridesmaids (Cont.)

Hire Details

Items to be hired_____   Cost £_____

Dates for fittings_____

Date for collection_____

To be returned by_____   Date for return_____

Deposit £_____   Date paid_____

Balance £_____   Date paid_____

Headdress

Style/flowers_____

Cost £_____   Payment details_____

Accessories

Shoes_____   Cost £_____

Hosiery_____   Cost £_____

Jewellery_____   Cost £_____

Checklist 19   Clothes for the Flower Girl

Supplier/dressmaker_____

Address_____

_____

Telephone_____   Fax_____

Email_____   Website_____

Dress

Colour_____

Style_____

Bodice/neckline_____

Waist/sash_____

Sleeves_____

Shape of skirt_____

Length/hemline_____

Embroidery/trimmings_____

Fabric_____

Lining_____

Pattern No._____

Size/measurements_____

Dates for fittings_____

Dates for alterations_____

Date for collection_____

Cost £_____   Payment details_____

Deposit £_____   Date paid_____

Balance £_____   Date paid_____

Checklist 19   Clothes for the Flower Girl (Cont.)

Hire Details

Items to be hired_____ Cost £_____

Dates for fittings_____

Date for collection_____

To be returned by_____ Date for return_____

Deposit £_____ Date paid_____

Balance £_____ Date paid_____

Headdress

Style/flowers_____

Cost £_____ Payment details_____

Accessories

Shoes_____ Cost £_____

Petticoat_____ Cost £_____

Jewellery_____ Cost £_____

Checklist 20   Clothes for the Pageboys

Supplier/dressmaker_____

Address_____

_____

Telephone_____ Fax_____

Email_____ Website_____

Colour_____

Style_____

Fabric_____

Lining_____

Pattern No._____

Size/measurements

Jacket_____ Cost £_____

Trousers_____ Cost £_____

Waistcoat_____ Cost £_____

Shirt_____ Cost £_____

Shoes_____ Cost £_____

Socks_____ Cost £_____

Tie/cravat_____ Cost £_____

Cufflinks/tie pin_____ Cost £_____

Dates for fittings_____

Dates for alterations_____

Date for collection_____

Cost £_____ Payment details_____

Deposit £_____ Date paid_____

Balance £_____ Date paid_____

Checklist 20   Clothes for the Pageboys (Cont.)

Hire Details

Items to be hired_____

_____

_____ Cost £_____

Dates for fittings_____

Date for collection_____

To be returned by_____ Date for return_____

Deposit £_____ Date paid_____

Balance £_____ Date paid_____

Checklist 21   Clothes for the Bridegroom

Supplier_____

Address_____

_____

Telephone_____ Fax_____

Email_____ Website_____

Colour_____

Style_____

Size/measurements

Jacket_____ Cost £_____

Trousers_____ Cost £_____

Waistcoat_____ Cost £_____

Shirt_____ Cost £_____

Hat_____ Cost £_____

Gloves_____ Cost £_____

Shoes_____ Cost £_____

Socks_____ Cost £_____

Tie/cravat_____ Cost £_____

Cufflinks/tie pin_____ Cost £_____

Wristwatch_____ Cost £_____

Total_____ **Cost £**_____

Payment details_____

Deposit £_____ Date paid_____

Balance £_____ Date paid_____

Checklist 21   Clothes for the Bridegroom (Cont.)

Hire Details

Items to be hired_____

_____

_____ Cost £_____

Dates for fittings_____

Date for collection_____

To be returned by_____ Date for return_____

Deposit £_____ Date paid_____

Balance £_____ Date paid_____

Going-away Outfit

_____

_____

Cost £_____ Payment details_____

Checklist 22   Clothes for the Male Attendants

Supplier_____

Address_____

_____

Telephone_____ Fax_____

Email_____ Website_____

Colour_____

Style_____

Size/measurements

Jacket_____ Cost £_____

Trousers_____ Cost £_____

Waistcoat_____ Cost £_____

Shirt_____ Cost £_____

Hat_____ Cost £_____

Gloves_____ Cost £_____

Shoes_____ Cost £_____

Socks_____ Cost £_____

Tie/cravat_____ Cost £_____

Cufflinks/tie pin_____ Cost £_____

Wristwatch_____ Cost £_____

Total_____ **Cost £**_____

Payment details_____

Deposit £_____ Date paid_____

Balance £_____ Date paid_____

Checklist 22   Clothes for the Male Attendants (Cont.)

Hire Details

Items to be hired_____

_____

_____

_____ Cost £_____

Dates for fittings_____

Date for collection_____

To be returned by_____ Date for return_____

Deposit £_____ Date paid_____

Balance £_____ Date paid_____

Checklist 23   Hair and Beauty

Weight

Present weight_____   Target weight_____

Health Spa

Name_____

Address_____

_____

Telephone_____   Fax_____

Email_____   Website_____

Dates_____   Cost £_____

Optional extras_____

Beauty Salon

Salon_____

Address_____

_____

Telephone_____   Fax_____

Email_____   Website_____

Appointments	Date and time	Cost
_____	_____	£_____
_____	_____	£_____
_____	_____	£_____

Beautician or Consultant

Beautician or consultant_____

Address_____

_____

Checklist 23   Hair and Beauty (Cont.)

Telephone_____ Fax_____
Mobile_____ Email_____

Details of treatment	Date and time	Cost
_____	_____	£_____
_____	_____	£_____
_____	_____	£_____

Hairdresser

Name_____
Address_____
_____
Telephone_____
Mobile_____ Email_____

Appointments	Date and time	Cost
_____	_____	£_____
_____	_____	£_____
_____	_____	£_____

Waxing *(full leg/half leg/underarm/bikini line)*

Salon_____
Address_____
_____
Telephone_____ Email_____
Date and time_____ Cost £_____

Checklist 23   Hair and Beauty (Cont.)

Manicure

Salon or beautician_____

Address_____

Telephone_____   Email_____

Date and time_____   Cost £_____

Pedicure

Salon or beautician_____

Address_____

_____

Telephone_____   Email_____

Date and time_____   Cost £_____

Checklist 24   Reception – Hotel, Restaurant or Banqueting Hall

Venue_____

Address_____

Telephone_____ Fax_____

Email_____ Website_____

Contact_____

No. of Guests

Day   Adults_____ Children_____ Total_____

Evening   Adults_____ Children_____ Total_____

Details of package_____

_____

_____

Hire Charges

Room(s) £_____

Exclusive use_____ Cost £_____

Times

Arrival_____ Evening reception_____

Meal_____ Entertainment_____

Speeches_____ Bar closes_____

Cutting the cake_____ Finish_____

Facilities

Room layout_____

Seating arrangements_____

Decorations_____

Display of gifts_____

Checklist 24   Reception – Hotel, Restaurant or Banqueting Hall (Cont.)

Marquee_____

Public address system_____

Changing room_____

Cloakroom/toilets_____

Car parking_____

Public liability insurance_____

Overnight accommodation   No. of rooms_____ Cost £_____

Flowers

_____

_____

_____ Cost £_____

Food

On arrival_____

Menu selection_____

_____

_____

Cost per head £_____

Special dietary requirements_____

Special menu/small portions for children_____

Evening reception menu selection_____

_____

Cost per head £_____

Serving the cake_____

Checklist 24 Reception – Hotel, Restaurant or Banqueting Hall (Cont.)

Drinks

On arrival_____

Served with the meal_____

Wines_____

Served with the cake_____

Served with coffee_____

Bar facilities_____

Prices £_____

Staff

Servers_____

Bar_____

Cloakroom_____

Gratuities_____

Equipment

Colour of tablecloths and napkins_____ _____

Candles/candelabra_____

Cake-stand/knife_____

Entertainment

_____

_____

Total cost £_____ Cost per head £_____

Deposit £_____ Date paid_____

Balance £_____ Date paid_____

Date of confirmation (sent/received)_____

Checklist 25   Reception – Hall or Function Room

Venue_____

Address_____

Telephone_____

Email_____ Website_____

Contact_____ Date booked_____

No. of Guests Adults_____ Children_____ Total_____

Details of Hire Charges

_____

_____

Times

Access for prepn./decn._____ Entertainment_____

Access for caterers_____ Bar closes_____

Arrival_____ Finish_____

Evening reception_____ Access for clearing away_____

Facilities

Licensing rules_____

Bar facilities_____

Room layout_____

Tables and chairs_____

Food preparation area_____

Display of gifts_____

Marquee_____

Public address system_____

Lighting, heating and ventilation_____

Checklist 25   Reception – Hall or Function Room (Cont.)

Changing room_____
Cloakroom and toilet facilities_____
Car parking_____
Public liability insurance_____
Decorations_____
Flowers_____

Entertainment_____
_____

Clearing Away_____

Total cost £_____ Cancellation fee £_____
Deposit £_____ Date paid_____
Balance £_____ Date paid_____
Date of confirmation (sent/received)_____

Checklist 26   Reception at Home

No. of Guests

Day   Adults_____ Children_____ Total_____

Evening   Adults_____ Children_____ Total_____

Times

Caterers arrive_____   Cutting the cake_____

Arrival of guests_____   Evening reception_____

Meal_____   Entertainment_____

Speeches_____   Finish_____

Facilities

Marquee_____

Name of caterers_____

Access for caterers_____

Bar facilities_____

Layout of rooms_____

Tables and chairs_____

Display of gifts_____

Cloakroom and toilet facilities_____

Car parking_____

Public liability insurance_____

Overnight accommodation_____

Staff/Helpers_____

_____

Flowers_____

_____

Checklist 26   Reception at Home (Cont.)

Decorations_____

Entertainment_____

Clearing Away_____

Total cost £_____

Checklist 27   Marquees

Name of supplier_____

Address_____

_____

Telephone_____ Fax_____

Email_____ Website_____

Contact_____

Size of marquee_____

Style of marquee_____

Style and colour of lining_____

Hire of marquee_____ Cost £_____

Type of flooring_____ Cost £_____

Tables and chairs_____ Cost £_____

Staging for cake, disco, etc._____ Cost £_____

Heating and ventilation_____ Cost £_____

_____

Lighting_____ Cost £_____

_____

Exterior floodlighting_____ Cost £_____

_____

Public address system_____ Cost £_____

_____

Power supply/generator_____ Cost £_____

_____

Access to house/covered walkways Cost £_____

_____

Checklist 27   Marquees (Cont.)

Date of setting up_____   Date of dismantling_____

Total cost £_____

Amount of deposit £_____   Date paid_____

Balance due £_____   Date paid_____

Theme_____
_____

Flowers_____
_____

Decorations_____
_____

Checklist 28   Self-catering

No. of Guests

Day   Adults_____ Children_____ Total_____
Evening   Adults_____ Children_____ Total_____

Times

Food preparation_____   Speeches_____
Arrival of helpers_____   Cutting the cake_____
Arrival of guests_____   Evening reception_____
Meal_____   Estimated finish_____

Food

On arrival_____
Menu selection_____

_____

_____

Special dietary requirements_____
Special menu/small portions for children_____
Evening reception menu selection_____

_____

_____

Wedding cake_____

Drinks

On arrival_____
Served with meal_____
Wines_____
Served with the cake_____

Checklist 28   Self-catering (Cont.)

Served with coffee_____

Bar facilities_____

Staff/Helpers	**No.**	**Cost**
Servers_____	_____	£_____
Bar_____	_____	£_____
Kitchen_____	_____	£_____

Food £_____ Drinks £_____ Equipment £_____ Staff £_____

Deposits £_____

Total £_____

Checklist 28 Self-catering (Cont.)		
Duties	**Time**	**Person Responsible**
Shopping	3 months	
Shopping	1 month	
Shopping	1 week	
Cooking	3 months	
Cooking	1 month	
Cooking	1 week	
Preparation	1 day	
Preparation	On the day	
Assembling the cake	On the day	
Setting up the bar	On the day	
Serving food	Day	
Serving food	Evening	
Serving drinks	Day	
Serving drinks	Evening	
Slicing the cake	On the day	
Clearing away	Day	
Clearing away	Evening	
Washing-up	Day	
Washing-up	Evening	

Checklist 28 Self-catering (Cont.)			
Equipment	**No.**	**Source**	**Cost £**
China			
Cutlery			
Glassware			
Tables and chairs			
Tablecloths and napkins			
Candelabra and candles			
Cake-stand and knife			
Water urn			
Coffee/tea pots			
Heated trays			
Condiment sets			
Glass cloths			
Refrigerators			
Freezers			

Checklist 29   Professional Catering

Name of caterer_____

Address_____

_____

Telephone_____ Mobile_____

Email_____ Website_____

Contact_____

Party-planning Service_____

_____

No. of Guests

Day   Adults_____ Children_____ Total_____

Evening   Adults_____ Children_____ Total_____

Times

Arrival of caterers_____ Evening reception_____

Arrival of guests_____ Bar closes_____

Meal_____ Finish_____

Cutting the cake_____ Clearing away_____

Facilities

Room layout_____

Kitchen facilities_____

Refrigeration_____

Delivery arrangements_____

Equipment

China_____

Cutlery_____

Checklist 29   Professional Catering (Cont.)

Glassware_____

Cake-stand and knife_____

Tablecloths and napkins_____

Candelabra_____

Candles_____

Heated trays_____

Tables and chairs_____

Flowers

_____

_____

_____

Food

On arrival_____

Menu selection_____

_____

_____

Special dietary requirements_____

Special menu/small portions for children_____

Cost per head £_____

Evening reception menu selection_____

_____

Cost per head £_____

Wedding cake_____

Checklist 29   Professional Catering (Cont.)

Drinks

On arrival_____

Served with meal_____

Wines_____

Served with the cake_____

Served with coffee_____

Bar facilities_____

Prices £_____

Staff

Servers_____

Bar_____

Cloakroom_____

Master of Ceremonies_____

Uniforms_____

Gratuities_____

Insurance

Terms for breakages_____

Costs

Food £_____   Drink £_____

Evening reception £_____   Service £_____

Gratuities £_____   VAT £_____

Total £_____   Cost per head £_____

Deposit £_____   Date paid_____

Balance £_____   Date paid_____

Checklist 30   Wedding Cake

Type of cake_____

No. of slices or individual cakes required_____

No. of tiers_____ Size_____

Shape_____

Colour and type of icing_____

Decorations_____

Professionally-made Cake

Supplier_____

Address_____

_____

Telephone_____

Email_____ Website_____

Contact_____

Delivery/collection date and time_____

Delivery address_____

_____

Delivery charge £_____

Cake stand and knife_____ Cost £_____

Total cost £_____

Deposit £_____ Date paid_____

Balance £_____ Date paid_____

Home-made Cake

Recipe_____

Checklist 30   Wedding Cake (Cont.)

Dates

Cakes made_____

Almond paste_____

Icing_____

Decoration_____

Date of delivery to reception_____ Time_____

Cake stand and knife_____ Cost £_____

Total cost £_____

Checklist 31   Entertainment

Entertainer (1)

Name_____

Address_____

_____

Telephone_____ Mobile_____

Email_____ Website_____

Contact_____

Total cost £_____ Cancellation fee £_____

Deposit £_____ Date paid_____

Balance £_____ Date paid_____

Times

Start_____ Finish_____

No. of breaks_____ Times_____

Entertainer (2)

Name_____

Address_____

_____

Telephone_____ Mobile_____

Email_____ Website_____

Contact_____

Total cost £_____ Cancellation fee £_____

Deposit £_____ Date paid_____

Balance £_____ Date paid_____

Checklist 31   Entertainment (Cont.)

Times

Start_____ Finish_____

No. of breaks_____ Times_____

Music

First dance_____

Special requests_____

_____

_____

_____

Special instructions *(type of music required, volume, tempo, etc.)*

_____

_____

_____

Checklist 32   Stag and Hen Parties

Stag Party

Type of party_____

_____

_____

Venue_____

Address_____

_____

Telephone_____

Website_____

Email_____

Date_____ Time_____

Number of guests_____

Transport arrangements_____

Hen Party

Type of party_____

_____

_____

Venue_____

Address_____

_____

Telephone_____

Website_____

Email_____

Date_____ Time_____

Number of guests_____

Checklist 32   Stag and Hen Parties (Cont.)

Transport arrangements_____

_____

_____

Checklist 33   Honeymoon

Honeymoon destination_____

Address_____

_____

Telephone_____

Email_____ Website_____

Dates_____

_____

Holiday company/travel agent_____

Address_____

_____

Telephone_____ Fax_____

Email_____ Website_____

Total cost £_____

Deposit £_____ Date paid_____

Balance £_____ Date paid_____

Departure time from reception_____

Transport from reception_____

First night destination_____

Address_____

_____

Telephone_____

Transport to departure point_____

Airport/station_____

Flight number_____

Checklist 33   Honeymoon (Cont.)

Check-in time_____

Time of arrival at destination_____

Departure date for return journey_____

Transport to departure point_____

Departure time_____

Airport/station_____

Flight number_____

Check-in time_____

Time of arrival at destination_____

Transport home from airport/station_____

_____

_____

❏ Passports/visas	❏ Toiletries
❏ Marriage certificate	❏ Cosmetics/nail polish
❏ Currency/travellers' cheques	❏ Shampoo/hair dryer
❏ Vaccination certificates	❏ Clothes
❏ Tickets/hotel vouchers	❏ Accessories
❏ Itinerary	❏ Jewellery
❏ Travel insurance policy	❏ Swimwear/beach towels
❏ Cheque book/credit cards	❏ Dressing gown
❏ Driving licences	❏
❏ Car documents	❏
❏ Luggage keys	❏
❏ Maps/guidebooks	❏

Checklist 33   Honeymoon (Cont.)

❏ Camera/video camera   ❏
❏ Films/flash unit/tapes   ❏
❏ Sunglasses   ❏
❏ Sunscreen/after-sun lotion   ❏
❏ First aid kit/insect repellent   ❏
❏ Salt tablets   ❏
❏ Contraception   ❏
❏ Medication   ❏
❏   ❏
❏   ❏
❏   ❏
❏   ❏
❏   ❏
❏   ❏
❏   ❏

Summary of Honeymoon Expenses

Accommodation_____ £_____
Travel_____ £_____
Transfers to accommodation____ £_____
Travel insurance_____ £_____
Taxis_____ £_____
Currency/travellers' cheques____ £_____
Passports/visas/inoculations____ £_____
TOTAL_____ £_____

Checklist 34   After the Wedding

People/Organisations to Inform of Change of Name and Address

Date sent

❑ Inland Revenue_____ _____

❑ Employer/DSS_____ _____

❑ Bank(s)_____ _____

❑ Credit card company(ies)_____ _____

❑ Shops/stores re account cards_____ _____

❑ Insurance company(ies)_____ _____

❑ Bank Registrar's Departments re shares_____ _____

❑ Premium Bonds/National Savings_____ _____

❑ Building society(ies)_____ _____

❑ DVLC re driving licence(s)/car registration
   document(s)_____ _____

❑ Motoring organisations_____ _____

❑ Car insurance company(ies)_____ _____

❑ Membership secretaries of any clubs,
   associations, etc._____ _____

❑ Mailing lists for publications_____ _____

❑ Magazine subscriptions_____ _____

❑ Mail order catalogues_____ _____

❑ Family Practitioner Committee re GP_____ _____

❑ Optician_____ _____

❑ Dentist_____ _____

❑ _____ _____

❑ _____ _____

Checklist 34   After the Wedding (Cont.)

❑ _____ _____

❑ _____ _____

❑ _____ _____

❑ _____ _____

❑ _____ _____

❑ _____ _____

❑ _____ _____

❑ _____ _____

❑ _____ _____

❑ _____ _____

❑ _____ _____

❑ _____ _____

❑ _____ _____

THE DIY WEDDING MANUAL
How to create your perfect day without a celebrity budget
LISA SODEAU

This book will show you that with a little bit of planning and preparation, it is possible to have the day of your dreams without starting married life in debt. It's packed with money-saving ideas for: stationery, flowers, transport, hair and make-up, photographs, food and drink, the reception and much more – including tips from real brides and over 100 budget busting ideas.

ISBN 978-1-84528-405-3

PLANNING A WEDDING RECEPTION AT HOME
CAROL GODSMARK

This book will enable you to plan a wedding reception at home either with or without a caterer. There's a lot to think about: hiring the marquee, making sure you have everything that you need on hand – the things you take for granted if the reception is at a hotel, such as loos, adequate electrical power, parking, a stage for the band and lots more. This book will make sure you cover everything you need so the day goes smoothly

ISBN 978-1-84528-295-0

HOW TO GET MARRIED IN GREEN
SUZAN ST MAUR

As the whole "green" subject becomes more and more complex – combining environmental, ethical and organic issues, some of which can be conflicting – it's getting progressively harder to work out how to make your wedding eco-friendly without ending up with a glorified mudbath. Yet, quite rightly, many couples now want their weddings designed to help keep our planet, environment, agriculture and employment ethics as healthy as possible . . . without compromising on style, glamour, quality and, of course, fun. In this book Suzan St Maur neatly unravels the increasingly tangled web of green issues relating to weddings; so that you can enjoy your wedding (and its planning) even more, because you know you're making a difference

ISBN 978-1-84528-270-7

WEDDING SPEECHES FOR WOMEN
SUZAN ST MAUR

'It's no longer just the men who get to speak at weddings – here's help for female speakers to plan their timing and content including jokes, poems and quotations.' – Pure Weddings

'The perfect gift for those special people who have agreed to be part of your special day.' – Wedding Dresses

ISBN 978-1-84528-107-6

THE COMPLETE BEST MAN
JOHN BOWDEN

'A valuable asset for the friend who didn't realise quite how much is involved in being his mate's best man!' – Wedding Dresses

'A lifesaver for a terrified best man.' – Pure Weddings

This handbook will show you how to become the perfect best man . . . a best man who knows how to combine the best of the old with the best of the new.

ISBN 978-1-84528-104-5

BE THE BEST, BEST MAN & MAKE A STUNNING SPEECH
PHILLIP KHAN-PANNI

'Essential reading, and a great gift for those preparing to stand and deliver on the big day.' – Wedding Day

'Gives you all the low down on how to go about delivering a speech that will hold and impress the audience . . . also contains all the etiquette and do's and don'ts for the wedding as well as tips on helping to calm nerves.' – For the Bride

ISBN 978-1-85703-802-6

MAKING THE BEST MAN'S SPEECH
JOHN BOWDEN

The essential handbook for every petrified best man. It reveals how to prepare and present a unique and memorable best man's speech, explains how to conquer nerves and gives you plenty of sample speeches, jokes and one-liners to make your best man's speech sparkle like vintage champagne.

ISBN 978-1-85703-659-6

MAKING THE BRIDEGROOM'S SPEECH
JOHN BOWDEN

This handy guide gives the bridegroom all the tools you need to make a brilliant, humorous, but sincere speech. The author, a professional speaker with over 20 years experience supplies a rich selection of stories, jokes and quotations which can be easily adapted.

ISBN 978-1-85703-567-4

FATHER OF THE BRIDE: SPEECH AND DUTIES
JOHN BOWDEN

As father-of-the-bride this will be a big day for you, too, with the speech playing an important part in the proceedings. You'll want to get it just right so that you speak from the heart but enliven sentiment with humour, and your speech is remembered for years to come – for all the right reasons. This book is packed with valuable tips and advice about conveying just the right messages to your daughter and her husband-to-be, understanding what is traditionally expected of you and making a memorable speech.

ISBN 978-1-84528-400-8

How To Books are available through all good bookshops, or you can order direct from us through Grantham Book Services.

Tel: +44 (0)1476 541080
Fax: +44 (0)1476 541061
Email: *orders@gbs.tbs-ltd.co.uk*

Or via our website
www.howtobooks.co.uk

To order via any of these methods please quote the title(s) of the book(s) and your credit card number together with its expiry date.

For further information about our books and catalogue, please contact:

How To Books
Spring Hill House
Spring Hill Road
Begbroke
Oxford
OX5 1RX

Visit our web site at
www.howtobooks.co.uk

Or you can contact us by email at info@howtobooks.co.uk